ORTHO'S All About

Floors
and Flooring

Written by
Martin Miller

Meredith® Books
Des Moines, Iowa

Ortho® Books
An imprint of Meredith® Books

All About Floors and Flooring
Editor: Larry Johnston
Senior Associate Design Director: Tom Wegner
Assistant Editor: Harijs Priekulis
Copy Chief: Terri Fredrickson
Managers, Book Production: Pam Kvitne,
  Marjorie J. Schenkelberg
Contributing Copy Editor: Steve Hallam
Technical Proofreader: Ray Kast
Contributing Proofreaders: Beth Lastine, Ron Lutz, Debra
  Morris Smith
Indexer: Barbara L. Klein
Electronic Production Coordinator: Paula Forest
Editorial and Design Assistants: Kathleen Stevens,
  Karen Schirm

**Additional Editorial Contributions from
  Art Rep Services**
Director: Chip Nadeau
Designer: lk Design
Illustrator: Dave Brandon

Meredith® Books
Editor in Chief: James D. Blume
Design Director: Matt Strelecki
Managing Editor: Gregory H. Kayko
Executive Editor, Gardening and Home Improvement:
  Benjamin W. Allen
Executive Editor, Home Improvement: Larry Erickson

Director, Sales, Special Markets: Rita McMullen
Director, Sales, Premiums: Michael A. Peterson
Director, Sales, Retail: Tom Wierzbicki
Director, Book Marketing: Brad Elmitt
Director, Operations: George A. Susral
Director, Production: Douglas M. Johnston

Meredith Publishing Group
President, Publishing Group: Stephen M. Lacy

Meredith Corporation
Chairman and Chief Executive Officer: William T. Kerr
Chairman of the Executive Committee: E.T. Meredith III

Photographers
  (Photographers credited may retain copyright ©
  to the listed photographs.)
L = Left, R = Right, C = Center, B = Bottom, T = Top
Laurie Black, 9TR
Carpet and Rug Institute, 30TL
Grey Crawford, 13TR
DeGennaro Associates, 7TR, 30TR
Colleen Duffley, 11CR
Edward Golich, 8TL
Bob Greenspan, 4LC
Wm. Hopkins Sr., 11TR, 11BR
InsideOut Studio, 16, 18, 20, 23, 24, 26, 27
Jon Jensen, 4-5BC, 5BR
Mike Jensen, 12CL
Jenifer Jordan, 6TL, 12TL, 28TL
Lynn Karlin, 14TL
Tom McWilliam, 4BL
Mohawk Industries, Inc., 4TR, 6BL, 30BL, 84
Pergo, Inc., 4TL, 8BL, 9BR
Ken Rice, 10BL
Eric Roth, 10TL, 14TR
Rick Taylor, 12BL
Philip Thompson, 6TR

All of us at Ortho® Books are dedicated to providing you
with the information and ideas you need to enhance your
home and garden. We welcome your comments and
suggestions about this book. Write to us at:
  Meredith Corporation
  Ortho Books
  1716 Locust St.
  Des Moines, IA 50309–3023

If you would like to purchase any of our home improvement,
gardening, cooking, crafts, or home decorating and design
books, check wherever quality books are sold. Or visit us at:
meredithbooks.com

If you would like more information on other Ortho
products, call 800-225-2883 or visit us at: www.ortho.com

Note to the Readers: Due to differing conditions, tools,
and individual skills, Meredith Corporation assumes no
responsibility for any damages, injuries suffered, or losses
incurred as a result of following the information published
in this book. Before beginning any project, review the
instructions carefully, and if any doubts or questions remain,
consult local experts or authorities. Because codes and
regulations vary greatly, you always should check with
authorities to ensure that your project complies with all
applicable local codes and regulations. Always read and
observe all of the safety precautions provided by
manufacturers of any tools, equipment, or supplies,
and follow all accepted safety procedures.

You can choose from more kinds of flooring today than at any time before. Laminate flooring (above and above left) looks like wood, stone, or other materials, and you can install it yourself. Wood (opposite page) remains popular, and engineered wood flooring can even be installed over a concrete basement floor.

Tile—from rustic pavers to mosaic patterns (left)—makes an attractive and durable surface.

Tufted carpet (below left) is usually professionally laid, but new methods and materials based on hook-and-loop technology make do-it-yourself installation possible.

Self-stick vinyl tile is easy to install, and resilient sheet vinyl (below right) requires only moderate skill to install.

FOUNDATIONS FOR DESIGN

Perhaps no other aspect of home remodeling is as rewarding as installing new flooring. The floor often sets the tone and feeling of a room—either as the dominant feature or as a neutral setting for furnishings and decorating elements.

The floor not only contributes to a room's appearance, it affects its comfort too. So you must pay attention to more than aesthetics when selecting flooring materials. Flooring must also be durable, practical, and appropriate to daily living—white carpeting throughout the house may not be the best flooring if your family includes preteens, dogs, or cats. And if you plan to install the flooring yourself, consider the amount of time you have available and your skill level when choosing material.

This book is packed with information that will help you select and install a new floor, starting with a survey of basic design principles to help you get the look you want. Later chapters show you how to plan and prepare for the installation. Illustrated step-by-step instructions show how to install traditional flooring favorites, such as wood, resilient sheet and tiles, ceramic tile, and carpet, as well as the newest manufactured wood and laminate products.

The first step is to learn as much as you can about flooring. This book will give you a good start. Also, ask friends what they like and dislike about their floors; clip photos of attractive floors from decorating magazines and put them in a folder—make one idea folder for each room you're redoing. Compare materials and prices at local floor-covering showrooms and home improvement centers; file material samples, brochures, and color chips in your folders.

As you review your collection of design ideas for each room, you'll probably notice similarities—certain colors, textures, and patterns that appeal to you. Consider these preferences along with the information in this chapter and the next, and you'll be ready to choose flooring that's just right for every room in your home.

A PRIMER OF DESIGN

The subtle pattern of this bedroom carpet is calming and relaxing. The colors in the carpet harmonize with the room and its furnishings.

Books and articles about interior design would fill a large library. But the basic information in these four pages will help you understand design principles and make good design decisions.

GOOD DESIGN

Interior design is the selection and arrangement of elements to create an attractive and comfortable living environment. Simplicity is usually a mark of good design, but it is difficult to achieve.

Creation of a design starts with a decision about how you want to use a room. You can then develop a style that corresponds to that use.

For example, a bedroom should probably be calming and restful; a dining room, comfortable and inviting; a children's playroom, colorful and active; and a kitchen, practical and organized. So you would want some rooms to have boldly stated floors, while in others you would want the floor to recede.

A neutral floor (above) acts as a background for the patterned furniture and draperies in this living room. Bold blue carpet (below) lends a soothing background color to this bedroom.

WHICH STYLE IS YOU?

Style generally falls into two broad categories—formal and informal. Formal styles are characterized by symmetrical patterns, straight lines, right angles, and geometric figures. Informal styles are based on curves, random or asymmetrical patterns, and natural forms. A formal room usually has an air of seriousness or propriety; an informal one might seem more hospitable or casual.

Within these general styles, you'll find design schemes that relate to eras, places, or architecture—French provincial, Art Deco, southwestern, and contemporary are a few. To conform to some styles, you may have to limit your flooring choices. In most cases, the principles presented in this book will help you select flooring to achieve the look you want.

COLOR

Color is the most powerful design element. It's usually the first detail we notice about a room and the one that most affects how we feel. To learn to use color effectively, familiarize yourself with these terms:

■ **HUE:** the pure color name—red, blue, and yellow are the primary hues or colors.
■ **VALUE:** the relative brightness of a color—the shade of gray it would appear in a black-and-white photo. Colors of lower value (darker ones) usually recede and make a room seem smaller. Those with high value (lighter colors) tend to stand out and make a room appear large and airy.
■ **SHADE AND TINT:** modified hues. A *shade* is darker than the original hue, as if by adding black. A *tint* is lighter, as if by adding white. Pink is a tint of red, for instance.

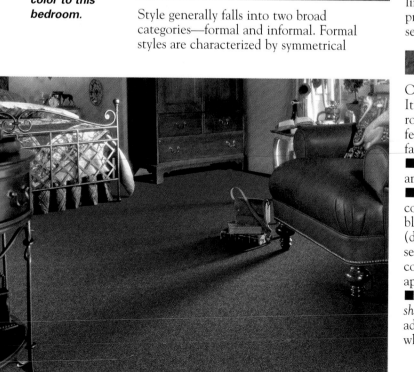

Color, pattern, scale, and texture work together to create a floor that either dominates the room or provides a background to the other elements. For example, highly saturated colors complement and harmonize with other hues of the same value. (Examples are dark walnut with blue tile countertops or pastel carpeting with peach walls). A color scheme with low contrasts lets other decorating elements stand out. Contrasting hues (white and black tile, for example) are forceful; they call attention to themselves. Black—the universal contrast—can make large rooms seem smaller.

Restraint is a good principle to follow when creating a color combination. Too much color harmony can be bland, and colors that are too dynamic can be unsettling.

COLORFUL CHOICES: When selecting colors, don't stop with the first one that appeals to you. You may find another one you hadn't thought of that will work better. For example, you might want a bright blue carpet, but after bringing home samples and looking at them on the floor, you see that a gray carpet with a subtle blue grid goes with your flowered sofa better.

If you don't want one color to dominate, sprinkle it throughout your design. A dash of your favorite color on black or white or on a neutral tone will tame it. For example, a striped turquoise border set around white ceramic tile won't overwhelm your bathroom floor the way solid turquoise would. You can find ways to introduce a color without making it the main attraction, even on a wood floor. For example, set off pine or stained cherry planking with a light-colored parquet pattern or with one or more accent colors stenciled in a border.

Colors can evoke moods too:
■ Reds and oranges call attention to themselves and create excitement. Tints of both colors create warmth.
■ Yellows and whites are cheery; they'll brighten up a dark room. However, too much of either may seem overpowering. Too much white can look sterile.
■ Greens and blues lend a calm atmosphere; deep tones hint at wealth, strength, and status.

Follow your intuition when choosing color. Modern trends in floor design favor muted or neutral colors, but don't be afraid to bend (or break) the rules to give a room its own distinguishing character and individuality.

A free-form tile layout in bold colors makes this hallway active and exciting.

FORM AND PATTERN

Form refers to the physical shape of the flooring material itself, such as square tiles or strips of hardwood. *Pattern* refers to a decorative motif—figures, shapes, colors— on the surface of the flooring.

Form and pattern greatly affect a room's mood and style. Small or understated patterns generally soften the mood of a room, but they can also lend an air of informality. Bold, active patterns can be formal or informal; either way, they make the floor a design element in its own right.

Form and pattern are closely related in flooring materials. For example, the form of solid and manufactured wood flooring (and many laminated materials) is linear and

CHOOSING A COLOR

These guidelines will help you choose a color for your new flooring:
■ Think of the color, not its name. Fanciful color names can influence you more than you think.
■ Trust your instincts—they reflect a preference for a certain color.
■ Take your time; a couple of days' consideration can help to make sure you've chosen the right color.
■ Narrow your choices to three or four. Take samples of each home.
■ If you're doing a complete makeover, cover the drapes, carpets, furniture, and fixtures so the colors you have now won't affect your new choices. Compare the samples with paint chips of the new colors as well as wallcovering and upholstery.
■ Samples will look slightly darker on the floor than in your hand. Set them on the floor and move them to different areas of the room.
■ Check colors at different times of the day and under different lighting. Sunlight will give the truest hue. Incandescent light adds a pinkish tone. Fluorescents may change the hue completely.

A PRIMER OF DESIGN
continued

The tile's rough texture lends warmth and informality to this breakfast nook.

rectangular; so is the pattern it creates. These board floorings can lend varying degrees of formality to a room, depending on the width of the pieces.

Solid wood strips (1½ to 3 inches wide) with an eased or square edge make a rich, formal-looking floor. Plank flooring (3 to 8 inches wide) looks more informal and serves well in rooms that have a rustic atmosphere.

The wood grain of strip flooring also becomes part of the design. Oak's highly figured grain, for example, weaves a random, active pattern across the floor, which can look dramatic and distinguished. Douglas fir's straight, plain grain, conversely, is well-suited to contemporary or informal rooms. Knots and blemishes in lower-grade woods (see pages 14–15) can enhance informality and reduce costs.

Parquet, which comes in square sections, forms geometric patterns on the floor. So does resilient (vinyl) tile. Parquet almost always creates a formal look, while the effect of resilient tile depends on the pattern of the tile itself and the arrangement in which you lay the tiles.

Ceramic tile carries the concept of designing with form even further. Tile shapes range from small square or octagonal mosaics to large, elaborately shaped pieces that can be combined in varieties to establish any look imaginable.

SCALE

Whatever the shape of the flooring, its size should be proportional to the room's dimensions to maintain balance. Similarly, the size of the pattern should fit the room. Just as a large lamp overpowers a tiny end table, a large flooring pattern looks unbalanced in a small room.

The scale of the pattern will make the room seem larger or smaller too. Large or busy patterns—especially those with several colors—usually make the room seem smaller. Busy patterns can be distracting, however, and may limit the number of ways you can redecorate the room if your tastes change.

Small patterns make a room seem larger. They also expand your choices in designing the rest of the room. You also should keep the form and pattern of the flooring in scale with other elements in the room design, such as the wallcovering and furnishings.

TEXTURE

Comfort and durability are the usual concerns when selecting flooring with a particular texture. But texture also affects the ambience of a room.

The rough and uneven surface of handmade pavers, for example, can give a southwestern or rustic feel to a room. For a more formal effect, lay down machine-made pavers that have a smooth surface. Glazed tiles usually brighten a room, while unglazed

A smooth and glossy surface like this marble-patterned laminate flooring supports informal or formal styles.

SCALE IN A NUTSHELL

These guidelines will help you make decisions concerning scale and pattern.
■ Large patterns make a room seem smaller.
■ Large areas generally call for large patterns; small areas need small patterns. Small patterns often become lost in a large area. Large patterns may overpower a small room.
■ The smaller the pattern and the more linear it is (stripes, for example), the more difficult it is to match at seams.

The geometric pattern created by the wood parquet flooring in this foyer provides a striking and formal first impression.

materials will soften the overall decor. A stone floor in a small, dark room may feel cool and inviting in the desert Southwest but chilly in coastal New England.

You'll find a wide range of textural variations in carpet too. Some carpet manufacturers offer the same style, color, or pattern in a variety of textures—heavy-duty, low-loop pile for the playroom or luxurious plush for the living room, for instance.

Texture also affects safety. Slick surfaces are dangerous at entryways, in kitchens, and near tubs and showers; a roughened surface helps prevent slipping on a wet surface. Consider how texture affects maintenance too. Smooth-textured tile and resilient floors are easier to sweep and mop than rougher textured ones. Wood and other materials may require protective coatings. Footprints, vacuum-cleaner trails, and lint show up more on uniform-pile carpeting than on carpeting with uneven pile.

THE DESIGN THEME

Creating formal and informal themes—or any style—depends on how you utilize the elements of design. Stripes, squares, and lines in carpet or resilient material can create a strong, formal look. A stenciled border on a plank floor can look cozy, even if it's in bright colors that command attention.

Floral or curved patterns will soften corners or unify floor space that might otherwise seem disrupted in a room with nooks and crannies. They will also look harmonious in rooms with curved spaces—under bay windows, for

example. Muted greens or blues will enhance this effect.

Random geometric patterns are often employed to add interest to a room with regular dimensions, square corners, and straight walls. If the patterns are in reds and oranges, or contrasting hues, the appearance can be even more dramatic.

Curves often work together to build a sense of motion; angular pattern elements oppose and hold each other in place; geometric pattern elements interact with one another to form an integrated field. An embossed texture in the pattern can highlight and punctuate that pattern.

Patterns also affect the perception of space within a room. If you extend a linear pattern along the length of a room, you'll make the room look longer and narrower. The same pattern arranged across the width of the room will make the room seem shorter and wider.

Laminated flooring in marble and wood patterns gives this entry an elegant look at an affordable price.

BE PRACTICAL

No matter how beautiful your new floor looks, it will satisfy you over the long run only if it proves to be practical. To pass the practicality test, flooring must meet these three standards:

■ It must be comfortable.

■ Its cost, including maintenance, must fit your budget.

■ It must be able to stand up to the traffic and activities in the room.

Hard floors can be made more comfortable. The rugs on this wood-plank floor provide comfort and define separate areas of the room.

COMFORT

Comfort, like style, usually is simply a matter of personal preference. Most flooring materials (except carpet and rugs) have hard surfaces. That's because they have to stand up to years of foot traffic.

Ceramic tile and dimensioned stone are the hardest—and the coldest—but you can warm them with radiant heating (see Radiant Heating at the bottom of the opposite page). Solid wood floors are hard, but some softwood species give a little more underfoot than hardwood species such as oak or maple. Cushioned resilient flooring has even more give, but not as much as laminate flooring, which is laid over foam underlayment. Carpet, of course, is the softest flooring.

Soft flooring helps control noise in a room. Soft materials absorb sound; hard materials reflect it.

COST

Choose the best flooring you can afford. High-quality flooring usually reduces long-term maintenance and repair expenses and helps enhance the resale value of your home. Cheaper or lower-grade flooring materials are often less durable. Wood flooring, however, is graded primarily on appearance, not strength, so lower grades may wear as well as higher grades.

LOCATION

In the real estate business, location is all-important. The same is true of flooring

You don't always need to install new flooring when redecorating a room. Paint inexpensively brightens the old wood floor of this sunroom that has been made into a playroom. The design incorporates board games and features a train track for the border.

FLOORS AND PETS

Consider your household pets—their comfort and the potential damage they can do to some materials—when you make your flooring decisions.

Ceramic tile and stone are the most impervious to claw scratches and damage from "accidents." Glazed tile cleans easily, but tile and stone may be less comfortable for pets to lie on.

Solid wood is not scratch or stain resistant, but a hard urethane finish can minimize the potential for damage. The finishes on most manufactured wood products are durable enough to fend off pet scratches.

Resilient sheets and tile—depending on their composition— fall somewhere between ceramic tile and solid wood in resistance to pet damage. Laminates are very hard—dogs and cats would probably find them as uncomfortable to sleep on as ceramic tile.

Carpet is the most comfortable flooring for pets and people, but it is also the easiest to stain. When you install carpet, you have to either really trust your pet or be able to respond quickly to remove any stains that occur.

If your pet sheds profusely, a neutral tone will camouflage hair between vacuumings. Tight-piled carpet will reduce the chances that pet claws will catch in it.

Whatever flooring material you choose, minimize problems by clipping your pet's nails regularly, sweeping the floor at least weekly, wiping up stains and spills immediately, and choosing water bowls with wide bases.

materials. Technological improvements have made almost all flooring materials suitable for any room and any use, but some continue to be considered better choices than others in particular rooms.

Entryways get a lot of use. Foot traffic brings in dampness and grit that will wear away a surface. Solid wood will provide a reasonably durable surface, but even polyurethane finishes for wood are not as hard and durable as ceramic tile.

Bathroom and kitchen floors must withstand moisture, so ceramic tile and resilient flooring are among the best choices. Textured vinyl tile tends to hide dirt, which makes it an excellent material for kitchens and playrooms.

Manufactured wood, laminate flooring, ceramic tile, and resilient materials are good choices for below-grade floors. And floor maintenance is not as complicated as it used to be. Most hard-surface materials require only periodic sweeping and damp mopping. Carpet comes (and usually stays) clean with regular vacuuming.

SAFETY

Consider safety when choosing your new floor. Resilient materials resist damage from moisture in bathrooms, for instance, but can be slick when wet. For safety, choose a resilient flooring material with a pebbled or embossed surface. Glazed ceramic tile is slippery when wet, so be cautious about using it on a bathroom or kitchen floor. If you do install it in wet areas, cover areas subject to spills or water with nonslip rugs. Lay nonslip rugs on hardwood floors too.

Resilient flooring is popular for kitchen and bathroom floors because of its water resistance. An embossed surface can improve traction and prevent slips when the floor does get wet.

Ceramic tile is an ideal low-maintenance floor in a kitchen or any room where there is high traffic or moisture.

Laminate flooring is easy to install and maintain. This pattern looks like a wood floor but costs less.

RADIANT HEATING

In a radiant-heat system, hot water flows through tubing in the subfloor, warming the floor which, in turn, radiates heat into the room. Water temperature in a radiant-heat system is cooler (80 to 125 degrees) than in hot-water heating systems with radiators. This keeps the floor temperature low enough to prevent damage to the flooring. You can add radiant heat to an existing slab by installing the tubing and pouring new concrete to cover it.

Although all flooring materials can be used with radiant heat, manufacturers' recommendations for installation over radiant systems vary. Check with your flooring distributor before choosing a material to cover a radiant-heat system. Here are some general guidelines:

■ Dry out a slab by turning on the system about two weeks before laying the floor and gradually increasing the temperature. Leave it at maximum for 72 hours, then turn it off for two days to cool down.
■ For glue-down floors (any materials requiring adhesive), ensure that both the flooring material and the adhesive are compatible with the heating system.

■ When installing nail-down flooring, make sure you don't puncture the piping when you drive in the fasteners.
■ The repeated shock of changing temperatures can damage some flooring. Ask your heating contractor about an outside thermostat. Installing one might prevent frequent temperature changes and help maintain more consistent flooring temperatures.
■ Carpet and pad may insulate the floor and keep the heat out of the room. Install carpet pads made specifically for radiant heat.

CHOOSING MATERIALS

Different flooring materials separate areas visually. The marble in this foyer makes an easy transition to the wood in the living room.

Ceramic tile lends itself to creative designs. Here, the floor's blue mosaic tile and the border pattern repeat on the walls and tub surround.

Combinations of standard materials can result in an attractive floor. Pine boards and Mexican tiles make up this kitchen floor.

Wander through any well-stocked retail flooring outlet and you'll discover a large selection of materials. At least one of them is bound to be ideal for each room in your home.

You'll find solid wood and manufactured wood flooring in different species. Some wood flooring comes prefinished so you can see exactly how it will look in the dining room.

The multitude of colors, sizes, and shapes of ceramic tile might inspire you to think about the geometric or free-form patterns you could lay out in a renovated bathroom or kitchen.

The display of carpet—a wide assortment of colors, textures, and sculpted patterns—might be where you find the perfect floor covering for the master suite, guest bedroom, or nursery.

And you're bound to see exciting colors and patterns in the resilients, either sheet flooring or tile, something that would go perfectly in the utility room or offer another choice for the kitchen or bath.

Recent innovations have improved the practicality, style, and affordability of all flooring materials. With few exceptions, most materials will work fine in most rooms today, *and installation has never been easier. Not long ago, a solid wood floor couldn't have been installed in a lower-level office. Manufactured strip or plank flooring makes it possible now— and you can install it yourself in one weekend. New technologies have made carpet longer lasting and more stain and moisture resistant. You may even consider carpet for the kitchen, and at a price you can afford.*

All the new choices mean you have to be prepared when you shop for flooring. That's how this chapter will help. On the pages that follow are descriptions of each material, design ideas, and tips on which rooms the materials

and ideas are best suited for. You'll also find out how each one is installed so you can decide whether to hire a professional installer or do the job yourself.

Plush carpet lends an air of comfort and tranquility to this living room without lessening its casual feel.

FLOORING MATERIALS—COMPARISONS

Material	Design Qualities	Uses/Rooms	Skill Level Required	Relative Cost	Durability
Solid wood	Strips and planks create linear and wood grain patterns. Wood tones. Parquet creates geometric layouts.	Popular in—but not limited to— dining rooms, living rooms, and entryways.	Requires moderate skill. Can cover minor irregularities.	High; slightly less costly than ceramic tile.	Durable, but can stain, dent, and fade. Can be refinished. Lasts indefinitely.
Manufactured wood	Same as solid wood strips and planks.	Same as solid wood. Can be installed below grade.	Easy to install. Some forms can cover minor irregularities.	Moderate; much less than solid wood materials.	Same as solid wood.
Resilient materials	Extensive variety of colors and patterns.	Versatile enough for any room. Excellent for kitchens and baths.	Generally easier to install than other materials, but will show unrepaired irregularities in subfloor.	Moderate; similar to costs for carpet. Solid vinyl and complex patterns increase costs.	Can dent, scratch, stain, and fade. Easy to replace.
Laminates	Variety of colors and patterns, including wood grains and ceramic tile look-alikes.	Almost any room that doesn't get wet.	Easy to install. Adapts to some irregularities in floor.	Laminate products are slightly more expensive than vinyl.	Resists dents, warping, rips, and scratches. Won't fade.
Ceramic & stone	Extensive variety of colors, patterns, and textures.	Suited for high-traffic or damp areas.	Layout and installation must be precise. Requires special tools.	In general, the most expensive floor covering.	Properly installed tile and stone is virtually repair free.
Carpet	Diverse colors and patterns. Softer texture than other flooring materials.	Popular for adding comfort to bedrooms, family rooms, and hallways.	Fairly easy, but requires special tools.	Moderate; dense fibers and complex patterns are more expensive.	Least durable of flooring materials. Can stain and wear.

SOLID WOOD FLOORING

Strip flooring is made in- 1½-, 2¼-, and 3¼-inch widths and establishes a strong linear pattern.

Parquet flooring in square tiles makes a geometric pattern.

The warmth, beauty, and durability of wood make it one of the most popular flooring materials.

Wood can add a feeling of quality, permanence, and livability to any room, and it will last the lifetime of the house if it is properly installed and cared for. The patina that comes with age only improves its appearance.

DESIGNING WITH WOOD

One of the first decisions about a wood floor is whether you want strips, planks, or parquet. Strips and planks make linear patterns. Parquet offers geometric options not possible with strips and planks. However, strip and plank flooring allows more flexibility than its linear form might first suggest. For example, boards lend

Planks are wider than strips—from 3 to 8 inches—and are often used in rooms with country themes.

themselves well to inlays and border designs. In addition, their directional nature can affect the apparent proportions of a room.

A long, narrow room will look more spacious if the strips or planks run across its width. A short room will appear longer if you lay the material parallel to the long walls. (Check the direction of the joists, however—strip and plank must run perpendicular to them unless you add additional underlayment and bridging.)

Although the color range of wood flooring is less than some other materials—ceramic tile, for instance—it is still broad enough to satisfy most design requirements. Colors run the spectrum from deep reds and browns through rich golden tones to almost white, and you can push these extremes by staining or bleaching. Or you can paint a wood floor in a solid color or pattern. Area rugs or larger carpets will add color and pattern to a wood floor. Rugs are an effective way to set off areas in large rooms with wood flooring too.

SOLID WOOD—INSTALLATION AT A GLANCE

Wood Frame Floor

Solid wood strips or planks

15-lb. felt

Joists

Plywood subfloor

Plank subfloor

Concrete Slab Above Grade

15-lb. felt

Solid wood strips or planks

Concrete Slab at or Below Grade

Solid wood strips or planks

15-lb. felt

Plywood subfloor

Moisture barrier

2×4 sleeper with insulation between

Moisture barrier

Plywood subfloor

Solid wood flooring is milled in two forms: tongue-and-groove, in which nails are concealed in a strong interlocking joint; and square edged, which you must nail through its surface. Both types of flooring require a solid subfloor, plywood underlayment, and a layer of felt.

Installed over a concrete slab, solid wood usually requires a moisture barrier for either plywood or sleeper installation. Insulation laid between sleepers suppresses noise and helps keep the floor warm on an unheated slab.

Grain in wood products provides textures that range from almost imperceptible to the fully figured patterns of red oak. How the board is sawn also affects the grain pattern. Plain-sawn stock (the least expensive) displays flat patterns along the length of each board. Quarter-sawn boards bear distinguishing cross-grain markings and perpendicular accents. They are the most distinctive wood products and the most costly.

FINISHED OR UNFINISHED?

Both solid and manufactured wood products come either unfinished or with a finish already applied. Choosing one or the other means balancing design with convenience.
■ Unfinished flooring (most solid wood products) lets you color and finish the floor exactly as you want. But finishing on site creates noise, dust, and delays in your use of the room.
■ Prefinished floors (most manufactured products) eliminate the mess, noise, and inconvenience of finishing the floor on-site. They come in a wide variety of finishes, but you are more limited in color options than if you finished your own.

SOLID WOOD EDGE PATTERNS

Tongue-and-groove square edge

Tongue-and-groove eased edge

Tongue-and-groove beveled edge

Plank square edge

Solid wood flooring is milled in thickness from ¼ to ¾ inch and widths from 1½ to 8 inches. Edge styles impart different design qualities to a room. A square edge is more formal and a beveled one more informal. Eased-edge flooring is somewhat less expensive and more usable over uneven floor surfaces.

WOOD FLOORING MATERIALS

Species	Color/Grain	Durability	Relative cost	Comments
HARDWOOD				
Red oak	Tan to light pink-red/ Highly figured	Very good	Moderate	Most popular species. Stains, finishes well
White oak	Light tan to yellow/ Straight to highly figured	Excellent	Moderate	Works and finishes like red oak
Ash	Light tan to white/ Straight	Very good	Moderate	May be special-order species
Maple/Beech	Light honey to white/ Fine and close	Very good	Moderate	Beech may be special-order
Pecan/Hickory	Honey to light pink/ Open grain	Excellent	High	Hardest wood flooring; may be special order
Birch	Light tan to white/ Open grain	Very good	Moderate	May be special order
Walnut	Dark red to light brown/ Fine to figured	Very good	Expensive	Not a stock species, special order
Cherry	Red to pink/ Moderately figured	Very good	Expensive	Not a stock species, special order
Mahogany	Dark red to brown/ Finely figured	Moderate	High	Not a stock species, special order
SOFTWOOD				
Douglas fir	Golden orange/ Straight	Fair	Inexpensive	Not a stock species, special order
White pine	Pale white/Open grain	Poor	Inexpensive	Not a stock species, special order
Yellow pine	Golden/Open grain	Fair	Inexpensive	Special order

SOLID WOOD FLOORING
continued

Choose wood species based on your design needs, your budget, and your room's wear requirements. Although grading terms vary for different species, the higher grades are generally more attractive and more expensive.

WHAT ROOMS FOR WOOD?

Deciding where to install wood flooring requires balancing aesthetics and durability. In a kitchen, for example, the contrast between warm wood and colder steel and plastic appliances and surfaces enlivens the room and provides a comfortable setting for family gatherings. But kitchens can be wet places, and moisture can damage wood flooring. To resist damage from standing water and spills, a floor must have a waterproof finish—usually polyurethane. Even with this protection, wood floors in kitchens need special attention and immediate action when spills and splashes occur. Acrylic impregnated wood flooring provides even more protection.

Living rooms, family rooms, and bedrooms, on the other hand, offer less-demanding flooring environments, even rooms that serve as multipurpose family areas. Rugs or carpets can protect wood from scratches and abrasion in places that get hard use. Rugs are also great for separating and delineating areas on a large expanse of floor.

Foyers and entryways cast first impressions, making them a perfect place for features, accents, and borders.

WHAT SPECIES IS BEST?

Flooring comes in more than 30 species, domestic and imported, hardwood and softwood. There really is no best species, but red oak is by far the most popular flooring. Other favorites are white oak, ash, cherry, and maple. Each species has its own specific color range, grain pattern, texture, and density, all of which contribute to the look and feel of the finished floor. Base your flooring choice on design qualities, costs, and durability.

The chart on page 15 compares the qualities of some of the most common species.

Don't be misled by the terms *hardwood* and *softwood* when assessing the durability of wood flooring. Those terms refer to botanical characteristics of the trees that yield the wood, not to the texture or density of the wood itself. Some softwoods are as dense and durable as other hardwoods. (Balsa, for example, is classified as a hardwood.) Some softwood flooring, such as pine, tends to dent easily. Most hardwoods will dent too. Fir or pine flooring develops a rich, warm patina with age.

GRADES

Grades differ by species. Oak and ash, for example, are graded as Clear, Select, Number 1 Common, and Number 2 Common. Maple, beech, and birch are identified as First Grade, Second Grade, Third Grade, or 2nd or 3rd and Better. For all species, grades are based on appearance; strength and serviceability are the same in all grades. Highest-grade flooring, which is nearly free of visual defects, costs the most. The number of blemishes allowed increases as the grade and cost decreases. Don't rule out the lower grades, however; knots, streaks, and spots in the boards can make a highly interesting floor.

BUYING AN OLD HOUSE WITH WOOD FLOORS

What could be more enticing than the patina of a well-maintained wood floor in an old home? Especially in a home you're planning to buy. But old wood can charm you out of your pocketbook after you move in. Investigate a bit before you sign the deal.

■ If the floor is carpeted, pull back a corner or two and check the condition of the floor.

■ If the seller doesn't want you snooping under the carpet, make sure your contract states who is liable for repairs or refinishing.

■ Look for pet stains (a smelly carpet is a sure sign of damage below it)—they almost always require replacement and refinishing.

■ Listen for squeaks, then look further. Squeaks might require only minor subfloor repair, but they could mean damage or structural problems you can't fix easily.

■ Determine what finish is on the floor (you may need a professional to do this). Some new finishes will not adhere to old coatings; most waxed woods will need to be sanded before refinishing.

PARQUET

PARQUET INSTALLATION

Parquet · Plywood subfloor · Parquet · Adhesive · Joists · Adhesive · Plank subfloor · Sealer or waterproof membrane · **Wood Frame Floor** · **Concrete Slab Above Grade** (Parquet not recommended for below-grade installation)

Parquet is usually wood tile manufactured for glue-down installations. It can be laid as shown here or in some cases, directly over solid wood flooring, resilient tile, or sheet flooring (but not on cushioned vinyl or no-wax surfaces).

Once beyond the means of the average homeowner—because the individual strips or *fillets* were cut and assembled by hand—parquet is now prefabricated, affordable, and easy to install.

DESIGNING WITH PARQUET

Parquet is manufactured in hundreds of patterns, each pattern determined by the arrangement and sizing of the fillets. It's a solid wood product, but unlike its strip and plank counterparts, it produces a nondirectional, geometric pattern. Because of this, and because it's made in almost as many species as solid wood strips and planks and in a number of shapes and sizes, parquet lends itself to fascinating design possibilities. You can even purchase individual fillets if you feel like creating your own design. You'll find parquet blocks available unfinished or in a number of prestained and finished styles.

PARQUET CONSTRUCTION

Groove · Tongue · Fabric mesh · Tongue · Spline · Groove

Parquet fillets are held together either by a fabric mesh, splines, or a lamination process. Some parquet blocks are cushioned and some are self-sticking. Parquet comes in both tongue-and-groove and square-edge styles, ranging from 5/16- to 3/4-inch thick and in squares, rectangles, octagons, and other shapes, from 4 to 12 inches wide.

ROOMS AND USES

Parquet does have its limitations. It's sensitive to moisture, so it doesn't work well in bathrooms or on below-grade floors. It must be laid over a completely dry subfloor. Parquet flooring fits into most decorating styles, though it tends to fit formal styles best. Properly sealed and finished, it will work in a kitchen. It makes a stylish surface for entryways and can bring elegance to living and dining rooms. Parquet would be a durable floor for a children's playroom too.

PARQUET PATTERNS

Block · Swirl · Herringbone

MANUFACTURED WOOD FLOORING

Manufactured flooring comes in two configurations— engineered and longstrip. Engineered flooring (above) is one board wide, no matter what its width. Longstrip materials (right) are usually three boards wide which allows you to cover more floor space in a shorter time.

Manufactured wood flooring has become one of the most popular products for do-it-yourself flooring. That's because it offers the rich appearance of solid wood in a form that can be installed by a homeowner over a weekend.

LAYERS OF WOOD

Solid wood throughout, manufactured wood flooring is constructed like plywood, as a sandwich of either three or five layers glued together with the grain of each layer running at 90 degrees to adjacent ones. The top layer, usually about $1/16$ inch thick, is the finish surface or *wearlayer*.

The layered construction results in flooring that is more dimensionally stable than solid wood strips and planks. This means it reacts less to moisture and humidity variations— it won't warp, cup, or buckle. This stability makes manufactured flooring a good choice for installation in damp areas or on below-grade slab floors.

LOWER COSTS, HIGHER WARRANTIES

Because only the top layer is visible, manufacturers can produce standard base layers of less expensive woods, changing only the top layer to meet the demands of their orders. That's why this flooring is more affordable than traditional strip and plank.

Manufactured flooring is graded for appearance based on the finish-surface species. Grades follow those for solid wood flooring of the same species. Manufactured flooring also has something that no unfinished solid-wood products do— a warranty. Warranties commonly cover the floor for from one to five years, but go up to 25 years for some materials. Some products can be sanded and refinished two or three times, depending on the thickness of the top layer. Although in most cases refinishing a manufactured floor is a job best left to the pros, some finishes require only light sanding to touch up a worn surface.

ENGINEERED OR LONGSTRIP?

New products bring with them new terminology. Manufactured flooring is made in two styles: single strips or planks, called *engineered* flooring, and planks with multiple strips (usually three) on their surface, called *longstrip* flooring.

Both styles are constructed with tongues and grooves and are cut to fixed or random lengths from 12 to 60 inches. Most manufactured materials come prestained and prefinished (which also shortens installation time), but some manufacturers produce unfinished products as well.

Not all suppliers and manufacturers use the same terms to describe their products, and the term *laminated* causes some confusion.

ANATOMY OF MANUFACTURED WOOD FLOORING

Manufactured wood flooring comes in thicknesses from $1/4$ to $9/16$ inch, widths from 2 to 7 inches, and lengths from 12 to 60 inches.

3–5 hardwood layers with grain running perpendicular to one another

Hardwood wearlayer

Manufactured flooring is a laminated product (layers glued together) but some suppliers also describe flooring made from synthetic materials, such as plastic laminates, as laminate flooring (see Resilient and Laminate Flooring, page 20). Talk to the flooring dealer to make sure you get the material you want.

DESIGNING WITH MANUFACTURED WOOD

The pattern of both engineered and longstrip flooring is strips and planks, so they share the same linear design characteristics as solid wood flooring. However, their lower cost can make exotic hardwood surface layers more affordable. Homeowners who had not considered such species as santos mahogany, Brazilian cherry, or teak in a solid-wood tongue-and-grooved floor might find such woods within their financial reach as manufactured flooring.

WHERE CAN I INSTALL IT?

Versatility is a key characteristic of these materials—they can go almost anywhere. You can lay them in kitchens and baths where concern about moisture would rule out solid wood (but don't let spills and water pool on

FLOORING THAT'S A GRASS

While the words *bamboo flooring* might call up visions of the reedlike material used in fences, this is not flooring made like grass mats. It is, however, flooring made from a grass.

Bamboo is a grass, not a tree, and as a flooring material it's making rapid headway as a new and environmentally friendly product—after harvest it regrows to maturity in only 4 years.

Manufacturers cut strips from mature bamboo stems that grow in excess of 6 inches in diameter. Processing the stems removes starch and makes them insect and mildew resistant. The material is kiln dried and laminated in a process similar to other manufactured flooring materials.

Bamboo flooring is available unfinished or prefinished. It sands and finishes like oak (and of course can be refinished), and it can be glued down or nailed down for installation, depending on the manufacturer. Some products are slightly less hard than oak and others are as hard as maple.

them). And if you've been looking for a way to convert the basement spare room into an office, this is the flooring you want—even if the current floor is covered with ancient vinyl. Begin any installation over a concrete slab by laying down a moisture barrier.

MANUFACTURED WOOD FLOORING—INSTALLATION AT A GLANCE

Manufactured strips or planks

Joists

Plywood subfloor

Plank subfloor

Wood Frame Floor (Glue-down installation)

Manufactured strips or planks

Foam underlayment

Moisture barrier or waterproofing membrane (may not be required)

Concrete Slab Floor (Floating installation)

Although some manufactured flooring can be nailed or stapled down, most is designed to be glued to an adhesive bed or to float on a foam underlayment.

Subfloor preparation for both methods is similar to that for other materials, but installation on a concrete slab generally requires a moisture barrier.

In a floated floor, the edges of the material are glued together (but not to the underlayment), locking the entire surface in a single unit (see Laminate Installation, page 23).

RESILIENT AND LAMINATE FLOORING

Resilients are made from a variety of materials. The most popular are vinyl sheet products and tiles. Their resistance to surface moisture and wide variety of designs make them ideal for kitchens and baths.

Resilient and laminate flooring combine appearance, durability, and ease of installation. Although no flooring is completely dentproof, resilients are able to withstand high compressive shock (dents from furniture, for example) without suffering long-term damage. Resilient flooring includes vinyl products, cork, and rubber.

VINYL SHEET AND TILE

Vinyl has long since replaced the old amalgam of linseed oil, cork, and wood that was called linoleum. (You can still special-order linoleum.) Likewise, vinyl has taken over the tile market from old vinyl asbestos tile (containing fibers that are a health hazard). The technological improvements have brought with them a number of different looks for flooring.

SHEET VINYL is manufactured in two forms—*rotogravure* and *inlaid*. The pattern is printed on the surface of a rotogravure sheet. A cushioned back helps hide imperfections in the underlying floor surface, and the sheet's flexibility makes it easy to install. Inlaid sheet goods are not printed; instead, vinyl chips are fused into the body material to make a pattern that goes completely through the

material. The solid pattern is less subject to wear than an imprinted pattern.

Both materials can be self-coved, curved, and extended up the wall for 4 to 6 inches to allow easy and effective cleaning in kitchens and baths.

VINYL COMPOSITION AND SOLID VINYL TILE differ in their manufacturing process and their vinyl content. Solid vinyl tile contains more vinyl, so it's more resilient—and costly. The pattern and color in both materials are integrated throughout, and both are available in no-wax finishes. Solid vinyl tile has more patterns to choose from, including some that look like hardwood, stone, and ceramic tile. Vinyl composition tile usually has self-stick backings.

CUSHIONED VINYL TILES are the thinnest (and least costly) vinyl tiles. They are made with a thin vinyl layer adhered to a foam backing. These tiles are soft underfoot, but dent very easily.

RESILIENT FLOORING MATERIALS

Inlaid Sheet Vinyl

Clear wearlayer

Inlaid vinyl chips and plasticizers

Backing

Rotogravure Sheet Vinyl

Printed layer

Gel coat

Backing

Vinyl Composition Tile

Vinyl chips and filler throughout

Solid Vinyl Tile

Vinyl chips and filler molded together by heat and pressure

RESILIENT AND LAMINATE FLOORING MATERIALS

	Solid Vinyl	Vinyl Composition	Rubber	Vinyl-Coated Cork	Laminates
Color, pattern, texture	Wide range of colors and patterns. Smooth or embossed surfaces.	Many colors and patterns. Solid and marbleized colors. Smooth or embossed surfaces.	Handful of solid and marbleized colors. Smooth, ribbed, or studded surfaces.	Limited range of natural cork colors. Smooth surfaces.	Wide range of colors and patterns. Surfaces are smooth.
Durability	Grease and oil resistant. Susceptible to heat. Medium- to heavy-duty gauges.	Good for damp areas, properly seamed. Good resistance to chemicals. Light-, medium- and heavy-duty gauges.	Good for damp areas. Resistant to most chemicals. Susceptible to grease and oil stains. Heavy-duty gauges.	Grease and oil resistant. Susceptible to heat. Cushioned, may dent. Medium- to heavy-duty gauges.	Very resistant to most kinds of damage, including stains and dents. Resists scratching.
Resilience	Good resiliency and sound insulation.	Not as resilient or sound insulating as solid vinyl.	Very comfortable underfoot. Good sound insulation.	Very comfortable underfoot. Good sound insulation.	Not resilient, but underlayment offers cushioning and sound insulation.
Maintenance requirements	Damp-mop or sponge-mop; avoid excess water.	Damp-mop or sponge-mop.	Damp-mop or sponge-mop.	Damp-mop or sponge-mop; avoid excess water.	Damp-mop.
Relative Cost	High.	Low to medium.	Medium to high.	Highest.	Moderate.

RESILIENT SHEET AND TILE—INSTALLATION AT A GLANCE

Because resilients are soft, they will show the imperfections of the subfloor. Smooth and fill the surface before laying the flooring. Many resilient materials are ideal for below-grade slabs. All flooring installation on a slab should start with a moisture barrier that is firmly adhered to the surface. Certain wood frame floors may also require a moisture barrier and should be at least 18 inches above ground.

RESILIENT AND LAMINATE FLOORING
continued

RUBBER AND CORK

Rubber and cork are made from natural substances that are able to bounce back from being struck.

RUBBER TILE is limited to only a few colors and patterns, but it is used more these days in kitchens because it is soft underfoot and its studded surface helps prevent slipping. Extremely durable and long lasting, rubber tile can last up to 20 years.

CORK TILE is made with a cork layer sandwiched between a vinyl backing and a clear vinyl top layer. Each tile is unique in color and the pattern of its pores, so it's easy to create a singular design. It also insulates against noise effectively.

LAMINATE MATERIALS

Laminate materials have been used for floors in Europe for almost 20 years. In North America, they are a recent flooring innovation—one that's made to order for today's do-it-yourself market. They provide exceptional durability with moderate cost (somewhat higher than resilients) and easy installation. Like manufactured flooring, laminates are made in layers, with an extremely hard top layer, or *wearcoat*, usually made of melamine impregnated with hardening resins. The wearcoat, which borrows technology employed in the manufacture of laminate countertops, is tough enough to withstand the impact of high-heeled shoes. As on laminated countertops, the surface resists damage from burns and stains. The flooring's pattern is printed on a film layer beneath the wearcoat. Laminates have tongue-and-groove edges. Some styles fit together with interlocking metal edges that can be unlocked later so you could move this flooring to a different room or take it with you to reinstall in a new home.

AN ARRAY OF DESIGN

Where a beautiful visual effect is the primary concern but practicality is still important, resilient flooring can meet both requirements while keeping the budget under control. Laminates are slightly more costly and come in slightly fewer styles.

You'll find classic resilient patterns reminiscent of the 1930s and 1940s, contemporary neutrals, and a rainbow of designer colors. Sheet materials come in many geometric patterns. Other patterns mimic other materials—ceramic tiles, pavers, cork, brick, and stone. Many laminate patterns look like solid wood, but you can find sandstone and marble patterns, abstract designs, ceramic patterns, and floral designs too. Many laminate products come in plank form. Planks that incorporate square-tile patterns are rapidly gaining in popularity.

Differences in form between resilients and laminates is another consideration when choosing either of them for your floor.

Sheet goods generally come in 6- and 12-foot widths. If the room is larger than the sheet width, you'll have to seam two pieces. Seam placement will affect the look and durability of the floor, so place seams in the least-used section of the room to make them less noticeable and less subject to wear. Joining sheets along a pattern line will make the seam less visible.

Seams don't pose problems with tile or laminate planks and boards. You can lay tile and laminate squares on a grid that's either square or diagonal to the walls. For added interest, set them in a border, a checkerboard pattern, or random designs.

Wood-strip and faux-stone laminate planks have a predominantly linear pattern.

ROOMS AND USES

Resilient and laminate materials can go in almost any room in the house and most are suited for below-, at-, and above-grade installations.

Resilients and laminates can create an expansive, elegant effect, whether they are glossy or matte surfaced, lightly mottled or highly textured, monochromatic or marbleized. The combination of elegance

ANATOMY OF LAMINATE FLOORING

Clear melamine wearcoat

Print layer

Bonding layer

High density fiberboard core

Melamine backing

and practicality makes either kind of flooring a good choice for an entryway.

An entryway floor should make a good impression on guests, yet be able to withstand the wear and tear caused by tracked-in dirt and water. If you choose a laminate plank with a solid-wood strip pattern, it could be difficult to tell it from the real thing. Cork flooring makes a striking entryway, too.

Resilient vinyl and rubber flooring resist surface moisture. This makes them ideal for kitchens and other areas where heavy traffic or high activity can lead to soil and spills. Rubber is also an excellent choice in a photographic darkroom, because it is especially resistant to chemicals. Laminates, though tough on top, are susceptible to moisture, so most producers advise against kitchen or bath installations.

Many bathrooms need the softening effects of warm-colored floors to offset the cool look of fixtures. Resilient floors come in a variety of colors to fit any style. The textured surfaces available on resilient flooring help prevent slipping—another important consideration for rooms where moisture is unavoidable and the floor frequently may get wet.

Easy-to-maintain resilient and laminate floors are just right for rooms that are used for play—children's bedrooms and family rooms. Brightly colored tiles, sheet goods, and laminates in lively patterns can enliven a playroom design.

Although resilient flooring installs easily, proper preparation of the subfloor is essential to ensure long wear. The high surface gloss of

Laminate planks are all about the same size—4 inches wide and about ¼ inch thick. They look like wood plank, wood strip, and a variety of stone and ceramic patterns.

most resilient materials will call attention to subsurface defects and irregularities. Unless you prepare a smooth subsurface, sooner or later traffic moving through the room will wear off the finish over these irregularities and wear out the flooring. If you cannot make the subsurface smooth enough, you should choose a different type of material.

Laminate boards come in a variety of sizes, from roughly 7-inch to 2-foot squares, with either a single pattern in stone, abstracts, and florals, or one that mimics tile, complete with grout lines.

LAMINATE FLOORING—INSTALLATION AT A GLANCE

One decision you don't have to make with laminate flooring, is how to install it. Laminates are laid over foam underlayment, with their tongue-and-groove edges glued together. The foam cushions the floor to make it feel more resilient underfoot, keeps the glue from adhering to the subfloor, and provides some thermal insulation.

Be sure to use the glue specified by the manufacturer or you may void the laminate warranty, which can be good for up to 25 years.

CONCRETE SLAB
Moisture barrier (required for below-grade and on-grade slabs. May be needed on above-grade slabs)

Laminate planks or tiles

Foam underlayment

WOOD FRAME FLOOR
Foam underlayment

Joists

Plywood subfloor. Some flooring manufacturers require vapor barrier

CERAMIC TILE AND DIMENSIONED STONE FLOORING

Ceramic tile and dimensioned stone have their origins in the earth, but their simple beginnings belie their versatility—and beauty—as flooring materials. The terms *ceramic tile* and *dimensioned stone* apply to a variety of products, some more suited to certain installations than others.

CERAMIC TILE

Ceramic tile refers to a clay product that has been baked in a kiln. As you search for the right tile for your floor, you will find these four types:

QUARRY TILE: These tiles are made from red clay and are about ½ to ¾ inch thick. They come in various sizes and shapes (4- to 12-inch squares and hexagons, and rectangles, usually 3×6 inches or 4×8 inches). Tiles can be either semivitreous or vitreous. (See "Water Absorption" on page 26.) The tile is made in natural earth tones—usually red—or can be tinted. Glazed tiles display a rainbow of colors and don't require sealing. Unglazed tiles must be sealed for protection against moisture and stains.

Ceramic tile and dimensioned stone are manufactured in a wide variety of sizes. Your choice of material size depends on the scale of the pattern you're designing, relative to the size of the room.

MORTAR BED

Installing tiles over a mortar bed is one of the oldest and most durable methods of tile installation. It's also the heaviest. If you want to set tile or brick in a mortar bed, make sure your floor can hold the weight.

If the original design of your home included plans for masonry flooring (which is unlikely) the building specifications would have allowed for the extra weight. In new wood frame construction, space the joists on 12-inch centers. If you're planning a tile or brick floor installation in an older home, you'll have to reinforce the floor to comply with your local building codes.

Once the floor is ready, anchor 1× float strips level with and parallel to each other in equal-size sections of the area. Trowel latex additive mortar (available premixed) between them, then drag a wood screed (a 2×4) across the float strips to level the bed. Fill depressions and rescreed, then let mortar cure for 24 hours before setting the tile or brick.

PAVERS: These handmade or machine-made tiles are generally ½ inch to ¾ inch thick. They may be made of any material from porcelain to nonvitreous terra-cotta. Machine-made pavers are made to precise dimensions in a range of colors and textures. Handmade pavers are usually earth toned and rough, which adds to their charm. Most pavers are square, but other shapes are available. Pavers come glazed or unglazed.

MOSAICS: Porcelain, clay, or glass tiles smaller than 2 inches, ranging from ³⁄₃₂ inch to ¼ inch thick, are called mosaic tiles. They are dense and vitreous, and almost always come mounted on a mesh backing.

PATIO TILES: These are thicker than other tiles—up to about 1 inch —and have irregular shapes and sizes. Most of these are unglazed and absorbent.

CEMENT-BODIED TILE

Cement-bodied tiles are made of mortar. Some are molded, others are cut or pressed from a sheet. The tiles are cured, not fired, which makes them less expensive than ceramic materials. Their appearance ranges from the rough appeal of unglazed Saltillo tiles to more costly faux-stone or ceramic surfaces and colorful decorative tile. They are not vitreous so you should not lay them in areas that might freeze.

CERAMIC AND DIMENSIONED STONE FLOORING MATERIALS

	Glazed (quarry, porcelain tile, mosaic)	Unglazed (quarry, porcelain, terra-cotta, pavers)	Cement-Bodied Tiles	Dimensioned Stone
Appearance	4- to 12-inch squares and hexagons (single tiles), 1- to 2-inch mosaics. Other geometric shapes. Rounded or squared edges.	4- to 12-inch squares and rectangles; other geometric shapes. Machine-made—uniform dimensions. Handmade—rustic appearance.	4- to 12-inch squares and rectangles. Often imitates quarry tile or stone, but appearance ranges from rough to sanded and colored.	12- to 24-inch squares and rectangles.
Colors and textures	Wide variety of brilliant and muted colors. Glossy, matte, or textured nonslip surface.	Natural earth tones, some blues, greens, and pastel hues. Matte or textured nonslip surface.	Earth tones to a wide variety of colors.	Unusual colors and veining, depending on origin. Glossy, matte, or honed (nonslip) texture.
Durability	Low to high, depending on method of glazing.	Machine made—high. Handmade—low.	Medium to high.	High.
Maintenance	Low.	Medium. Unglazed tiles require sealing and periodic resealing to resist stains. May be waxed.	Low to medium; depends on density. Requires periodic sealing.	Most should be sealed for best wear. Sealing darkens slate. Waxing is unnecessary.
Relative Cost	Medium to very high.	Medium to high.	Low.	Medium to very high.

DIMENSIONED STONE TILE

Dimensioned stone tile may either be cut from solid stone and polished or molded from a mix of stone chips and resins. Cut stone can be honed to give it a rougher and slip-resistant surface. You can install both types of stone tile in any locations suitable for ceramic tiles, using the same methods.

Although many types of stone are used, the most popular are marble, granite, and slate. The vitreosity of stone varies—marble is porous, but granite is usually dense. Stone tile requires an absolutely flat subsurface and must be handled carefully to avoid breakage.

Twelve-inch squares are the most common size, but you'll find squares up to 24 inches as well as smaller cut tiles. (You can cut smaller tiles yourself from larger ones.) Stone weighs substantially more than a ceramic tile of the same size. A ⅜-inch-thick stone tile can weigh close to 6 pounds per square foot. Stone is a classic flooring material, but it is expensive and—because it's heavy and can crack easily—difficult to install.

CERAMIC TILE AND DIMENSIONED STONE— INSTALLATION AT A GLANCE

On Wood Frame Floor
Waterproof or isolation membrane (if necessary)
Thinset for membrane
Cement backerboard
Thinset for backerboard
Plywood subfloor
Thinset for tile
Tile

Waterproof or isolations membrane (if necessary)
Thinset for membrane
Thinset for tile
Tile
On Concrete Slab

Most tile and stone floors can be installed with thinset mortar. Backerboard provides stability on wood frame floors, but is not required on concrete slabs. Some installations call for waterproof and isolation membranes—one keeps out moisture and the other allows materials to expand at different rates without cracking the tile.

CERAMIC TILE AND DIMENSIONED STONE
continued

IT LOOKS GOOD, BUT...

Tile might look beautiful but not be manufactured to high quality standards. Colorful or elaborately patterned tiles can be as inferior as plain tiles. Density and vitreosity make the difference between high-quality tiles and what the industry classifies as rubbish (tiles with a water absorption rate of 7 percent or more).

TILE GLAZES

Glazes made of lead silicates and pigments are brushed or sprayed onto the surface of the bisque (the tile body) to add color and protect the surface of the tile. Glaze can be applied to the raw bisque before it is fired, or it can be applied to fired tiles, which are then fired again. Glaze gives glazed tiles their color. Unglazed tiles get their color solely from the clay. Additives are sometimes mixed with the glaze to add texture as well.

Glazed ceramic tiles are water-resistant. The grout lines between them are not—unless they are carefully sealed. Unglazed surfaces are water permeable and should be sealed against water absorption.

GRADING SYSTEMS

Ceramic and natural stone are graded according to their quality. Familiarizing yourself with these grades will help when choosing the right tile for your room.

CERAMIC TILE GRADES:
- **Group 1:** Tile suitable for bathrooms with little foot traffic.
- **Group 2:** Suitable for residential use, but not in heavy-traffic areas, such as kitchens and entrance halls.
- **Group 3:** Suitable for all residential areas.
- **Group 4 & 5:** Tiles suitable for various commercial applications.

DIMENSIONED STONE GRADES:
- **Group A:** Uniform and consistent. You can work these tiles without much fear of breaking them.
- **Group B:** Similar to Group A, but more prone to breakage and surface damage.
- **Group C:** Natural variations may increase likelihood of breakage.
- **Group D:** Often the most beautiful, but also the most likely to break or be damaged.

DESIGNING WITH TILE

No other material offers the design possibilities of tile. With tile, you can control color, form, pattern, scale, and texture.

Your design scheme can draw the eye to a focal point with vivid colors. Or you can rely on a monochromatic scheme to unify other colors in the room. You could repeat different shapes and colors to create an overall motif and rejuvenate a single-colored room or border a checkerboard pattern with contrasting colors, patterns, and shapes. Another option would be to make the checkerboard itself with three or more colors or different glazes.

Your floor can be dignified or bold, quiet or dramatic. Put a floral-and-fruit pattern in

Glazed tiles will brighten a room with their limitless hues and shades. Color is a versatile element, but it must be used with caution to keep it from overpowering the room.

WATER ABSORPTION

Tile varies in its vitreosity—its ability to resist water absorption.

Nonvitreous tile is absorbent. It can absorb more than 7 percent of its weight in water and is not suitable for installations where it will get wet or freeze.

Semivitreous tile has an absorption rate of 3 to 7 percent—not water resistant enough for outdoor use.

Vitreous tile absorbs only .5 to 3 percent of its weight in water, and is ideal for use in almost any location. It's also denser, which makes it stronger.

For most flooring installations, select a tile that resists water—an impervious or vitreous tile. In certain cases, nonvitreous and semivitreous tile will work. Ask your distributor about the vitreosity of a tile and its suitability for your proposed use before you purchase it.

Although the tiles seen most commonly are square, tiles are cut in octagons, hexagons, rectangles, and triangles. You can cut triangles yourself from squares or rectangles.

Texture plays an important role in tile installations. Rough textures provide traction and tend to mute colors. Glossy textures are slick and create or augment modern themes.

the kitchen to celebrate nature's bounty or use stark geometrics if efficiency is desired look.

Recreate a turn-of-the-century interior with 2-inch mosaics. Make the entry to your family room feel like a villa by weaving tiles in an offset pattern. Separate the entry from the living room with a ceramic tile grid. Or use dimensioned stone for a great first impression.

Small tile or small patterns will blend together in a large room to create a single pattern across the floor; large tiles will appear as distinct units. Large tiles will jump out in a small room, smaller tiles will look quiet.

WHERE TO USE TILE

Ceramic and dimensioned stone tile can be used in any room of the house. Tile is a traditional floor surface for kitchens and bathrooms, but be sure you choose a vitreous tile for these installations. Nonslip textures offer additional safety. Unglazed tile does not resist water or staining well enough for use in a kitchen unless you seal it. Use glazed tiles with a matte finish around showers and tubs. Coordinate the decor with the same tile on tub and shower surrounds and on vanities. A family room is another great place to put tile; messes caused by pets, children, or party guests clean up easily. Tiles installed around fireplaces and hearths unify the appearance of the room as well.

Ceramic and stone tiles feel cool to the touch, an advantage in hot weather but not in cold climates. Where the weather gets cold, you can install tile over radiant heating or let it collect solar heat.

WATCH YOUR WEIGHT

The weight of a tile installation—even one installed on a thinset bed—can overstress a wood frame floor enough so you may have to reinforce it to comply with local codes. If you are in doubt about your floor's capacity, consult an architect, builder, or engineer.

Tile thickness will raise the floor level. This may make a tile surface impractical where floor levels are established, where the raised level will interfere with cabinets and appliances, and where raised transitions to other rooms might be awkward. To ease the height difference between different materials, install transitions made especially for this purpose.

The pattern of a tile installation comes from both the individual tiles and the repeated figures (color, texture, shape, and size) throughout the design.

CARPET

Texture affects the look of a carpeted room. Here, the carpet's sculpted pattern adds dimension to the otherwise neutral background.

W ith its wide range of colors, fibers, and textures, carpet is the most luxurious of flooring materials. The higher and denser the pile and the thicker the pad, the warmer and quieter the floor is to walk on. Like other flooring materials, carpet comes in a number of grades and qualities and a wide variety of materials. Do your homework before making your final choice.

Before you buy, obtain as much information as possible and compare claims and prices. These pages will tell you about different carpet fibers (see chart below right) and piles (see "Styles and Textures" *on page 31*). Some fibers age better than others. The best carpets are made of wool, but modern synthetic fibers combine quality with affordability.

Consider density—the number of yarns per square inch—when you shop for carpet. Generally the more yarn per square inch, the more durable the carpet. Ask friends whether they are pleased with their carpet. Is it wearing well? Is it easy to clean? Has it faded in the sunlight?

HOW IS IT MADE?

The variety of carpet can seem intimidating at first. A look at three of the most common manufacturing techniques will clarify things. **WOVEN CARPET** is similar to a hand-woven rug in that pile material is woven into an integrated backing. Woven carpet won't come apart at the layers and won't snag as easily as others. Woven carpet ranks highest in quality and cost.

TUFTED CARPET is made by sewing loops of pile material through a backing material (the primary backing), which then gets a coat of latex to keep the yarn in place. A secondary backing gives the carpet its stability. This process is extremely cost effective.

NEEDLE-PUNCHED manufacture uses barbed needles to punch the pile through a mesh backing. The pile is locked in and is difficult to unravel, making this kind of carpet ideal for outdoor installations.

CARPET INSTALLATION AT A GLANCE

Conventional carpet

Cushion-backed carpet

Pad (taped at seams)

Tackless strip

Plywood subfloor

Adhesive

Plywood subfloor

Carpet over Wood Frame Floor
(Installation is essentially the same over a concrete slab).

Installation varies depending on whether the carpet is conventional (with a separate pad) or cushion-backed (with a pad attached to the backing). Conventional carpet requires tackless strips around the perimeter to keep it in place. The pad is laid loose on a wood floor or taped to a slab. Cushion-backed carpet is glued to the floor.

HOOKS AND LOOPS

Manufacturers have taken the hook-and-loop fasteners popular in children's and sports attire to a new level: They've put it on the floor. Hook-and-loop technology eliminates not only tackless strips, but also seaming irons and heat-sensitive tape. The beauty of this carpet is that if you make a mistake, you can lift up the carpet and start all over. And no adhesives means no fumes or odors.

To install this carpet, first press the hook-and-loop tape around the perimeter of the room, leaving its protective cover in place. Then cut the carpet to the exact dimensions of the room (no need for surpluses here), and mark seam locations on the floor.

Dry-lay the carpet in place and butt the seam edges together. Carefully run a pencil line down the center of the seam to mark its location on the floor. Fold both seam edges back and press the 4-inch seam tape to the floor, centered on your mark. Roll the tape to adhere it. Then remove the protective cover on the seam tape, press the seam edges into it and roll the seam. Fasten the edges the same way.

CARPETS AND ALLERGIES

Carpet materials—backings, fibers, dyes, and other products used in its construction—may contain substances that some people are allergic to. Here are some ways to minimize discomfort during installation of new carpet.
■ Purchase carpet and adhesives that meet industry standards for low total volatile organic compound emissions.
■ Increase the fresh air ventilation during installation and afterwards for 48–72 hours.
■ If possible, unroll carpet and let it air out for two to three days before installing it.
■ Vacuum your old carpet before you remove it. Then vacuum the floor or subfloor after taking up the carpet and pad.
■ Remove loose fibers with a vacuum.
■ Keep humidity below 65 percent and vacuum regularly to minimize mite allergens.

THE BACKING MAKES A DIFFERENCE

The quality of the backing will not affect the installation of your carpet, but it will make a difference in maintenance and longevity. Look for a tighter weave (top, at right). A tighter weave usually means that the carpet is denser, more durable, and will stand up better to soils than a carpet with a loose weave (bottom).

COMPARISON OF CARPET MATERIALS

Material	Resilience	Staining	Abrasion	Fading	Mildew	Cost
Wool	Excellent. Feels springy underfoot.	Very good, but may be difficult to clean.	Very good.	Damaged by long exposure to sunlight.	Requires treatment.	High.
Nylon	Very good. Resists crushing.	Very good. More easily cleaned than wool.	Very good.	Damaged by long exposure to sunlight.	Excellent.	Medium to high.
Polyester	Fair. susceptible to crushing.	Fair. Cleans well.	Excellent.	Damaged by long exposure to sunlight.	Requires treatment.	Low to medium.
Acrylic	Good. Almost as good as wool.	Good, but must be treated after deep cleaning.	Poor.	Good.	Excellent.	Low to medium.
Polypropylene olefin	Varies with construction and type of pile.	Very good. Doesn't retain dirt.	Very good.	Treated to resist fading.	Excellent.	Low.

CARPET
continued

Carpet unifies this bedroom by incorporating the colors of its furnishings and wallcovering.

This traditional floral pattern will remain stylish for as long as the carpet lasts.

Most of the carpet installed today is tufted carpet made from synthetic material. Carpet also comes with a separate pad (conventional carpet) or with a pad adhered to its backing (cushion-backed carpet).

CARPETS IN DESIGN

A broad expanse of carpet pulls the room together and creates a simple sweep of color, pattern, and texture. Make these features work with—not against—each other. If bold color is important, choose an unsculpted texture and a simple pattern. If you want texture or pattern to be a dominant feature, choose a color that recedes. Soft, organic figures, plants, and leaves go well with other patterns. So do blues and water greens. Thick piles can soften geometric designs.

Textured carpet in a soothing green adds to the casual, relaxing atmosphere of this family room.

A bright, vivid color may be eye-catching on the swatch, but be careful! On a floor of any size, it might overwhelm you. Neutral colors, such as beige, taupe, cream, celadon, and gray provide a versatile background that does not conflict with the overall interior design scheme. They also adapt to changes in room decoration. You'll find them sprinkled throughout other neutral backgrounds in today's carpet designs.

PICKING PATTERNS

Patterned carpet is a textile, so it can have variations in the consistency of the pattern size, configuration, and match from one section to another. Fortunately, manufacturers have established tolerances and instructions that will result in an error-free installation. However, patterned carpet installation is best left to the pros. Here are some things to keep in mind when you contract the job.
■ Use the same criteria for choosing a carpet pattern as you would any other flooring material (see pages 6–11).
■ Installing patterned carpet requires more time and expertise than an unpatterned one—installation costs will be higher.
■ Exact pattern matches are seldom guaranteed, but the eye will not detect variations if the installer follows the manufacturer's instructions. Take your time in choosing a contractor—check references and certifications.

THE LABEL TELLS THE STORY

When you've narrowed your choices down to three or four, check the label on the back of the carpet sample. It tells what the carpet is made of, the width it comes in, warranty details, and its performance rating, based on industry standards.

The performance rating is based on a 5-point scale. A rating of 4 or 5 is best for high-traffic areas. A 2 to 3 will work fine in rooms with less traffic.

Always choose the highest quality carpet you can afford. High-density carpet like this will stand up to heavy traffic and look new for years. The pattern adds impact in this room.

If you want a lively accent, look for carpet with bowed patterns or swirls, plaids, and dots. You can find them in cut-and-loop carpets or multilevel loops. The texture of these piles doesn't detract from the pattern, it adds to the feeling of quality.

Carpet pile—whether looped, cut, or sculptured—runs in a definite direction, or nap. To get the best visual effect of color and texture as you enter the room, install carpet with the pile leaning toward the doorway.

A CARPET FOR EVERY ROOM

Be practical when choosing carpet. Think of the worst things that can happen in your home—muddy shoes, fireplace sparks, spilled cranberry juice—and plan accordingly.

Pattern can help disguise stains. A hard, high-density carpet with a small pattern wears well in heavy-traffic areas, such as kitchens and entrances. It helps camouflage inevitable stains, marks, and scuffs. Select fibers that resist moisture and mildew. For a family room, you'll want a carpet that resists stains and spills but feels soft enough to sit or lie on.

Carpet can make a bathroom cozier, taking the cold edge off of slick surfaces. You can install tile around the shower, washbasin, and tub, and moisture and mildew resistant carpet on the drier sections of the floor.

A single sweep of soft carpet makes the bedroom a more inviting place. It adds warmth on cold mornings and cuts down on noise. Carpet will also reduce noise of stairways and hallways too.

STYLES AND TEXTURES   *The style of the pile affects both a carpet's durability and its looks. Here are profiles of some of the more popular styles.*

Saxony: smooth, formal, velvety; shows footprints.

Cut and loop: Multi-colored surface looks carved, hides stains.

Textured saxony: casual, hides footprints.

Multilevel loop: casual, hides footprints; durable.

Velvet cut: elegant, shows footprints.

Level loop: casual and durable, ideal for basement family rooms.

GETTING READY

Preparation and planning are crucial to a successful floor installation. The new flooring will be only one of several layers that make up the floor, and a relatively thin one at that. The flooring's durability and appearance will depend greatly on the foundation under it.

This chapter will acquaint you with the basic steps in planning your project, estimating materials, and installing or preparing a subfloor that will properly support your new flooring. First, you'll find information to help you decide whether you want to contract some (or all) of the job out to a professional, or whether you want to do it yourself.

The first question you should ask is: "Do I really want to do this myself?" The answer is often not easy. Doing it yourself will almost always save money. But cost is only one factor in the decision.

D.I.Y. OR CONTRACT IT?

If you're accustomed to doing home-improvement projects, you'll probably want to tackle your new flooring too. Doing the job yourself will probably save money, although your savings might be less if a contractor includes labor costs in the price of materials. Generally, the less expensive the materials and the higher the labor cost, the more you will save doing the job yourself.

DEALING WITH THE PROS

If you can't decide how you want your room to look, get some help from an interior designer. Interior designers are trained to help you choose design ideas and materials. Even an hour or so with a designer can quickly get you over design hurdles that you might otherwise wrestle with for days. Many home centers and flooring dealers have designers on staff who can help you, often at no charge. Independent designers are listed in the phone directory.

Once you've chosen your materials, you can start planning the installation. Dealers and installers can help you make decisions about installation. But make a list of questions to ask before you contact them. Here are some things you might want to ask:

ASK THE DEALER:
■ Does the material have characteristics that will affect installation?
■ What does the warranty cover, and for how long? Does it specify installation techniques?
■ Do material costs include installation?
■ Can required special tools be borrowed or rented with purchase?

ASK THE INSTALLER:
■ Are costs for moving and replacing furnishings included in the bid?

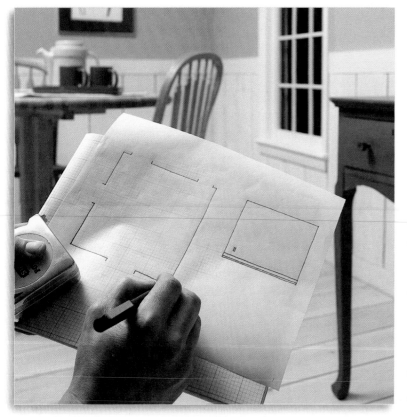

■ How long will the installation take?
■ Are disposal costs included?
■ What is guaranteed and for how long?
  When consulting with a dealer or installer, take along a copy of your dimensioned drawing. Suppliers can accurately estimate costs from it, and an installer will need a copy if he or she is to give you an accurate bid. Once you've gotten information from all sources, plug them into a chart like the one below. But remember—savings represent only one side of the equation. Even if you have the skills to lay wood flooring or ceramic tile, you may want to contract the job out if you have only one weekend available to do the project.

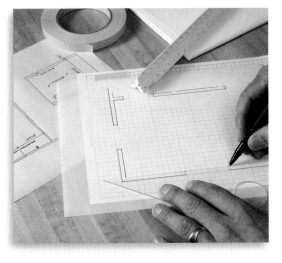

A scale drawing of the room makes planning easier. Start by making a rough sketch, shown on the opposite page. Then take measurements of the room and add them to your sketch. Redraw the room layout on graph paper to create your planning drawing.

CONTRACTOR/D.I.Y. COST COMPARISON

If you decide to do the job yourself, you'll probably save money on materials and labor costs, but you'll take more time to do the job than a pro would. To compare contracted versus do-it-yourself costs, itemize each of the elements shown below. Then consider the D.I.Y. skill level required to do the work and the time you have available.

Contractor costs

1. Subfloor preparation:	
Materials	$
Labor	$
2. Installation:	
Materials	$
Labor	$
3. Additional costs:	
Moving furniture	$
Delivery	$
Finishing, trimming, disposal	$
Total contractor costs	$

Do-It-Yourself costs

1. Underlayment costs:	$
2. Flooring material costs:	$
3. Tools to buy (list):	$
4. Tools to rent (list):	$
5. Supplies:	
Adhesive	$
Grout or wood filler	$
Nails or screws	$
Sealers, stains, finishes	$
Tackless strip for carpet	$
Baseboards, thresholds	$
Other	$
Total D.I.Y. costs	$

PLANNING CHECKLIST

Use this checklist to keep your flooring project organized from start to finish.
■ Measure all rooms carefully and calculate their areas.
■ Create a scale drawing of the rooms where you plan to install new flooring. Include all dimensions.
■ Estimate material quantities, starting with underlayment and other materials required for preparation—adhesives, grouts, tackless strips, and fasteners. Using the area of each room, estimate the amount of any finishing materials you will need.
■ Make a list of the tools you'll need. Purchase or rent them.
■ Estimate your total costs and do some comparison shopping for the best deals.
■ Make a contingent living plan, including the temporary relocation of furniture and anything else you can do to keep disruptions in your life to a minimum.

REQUIRED SKILL LEVELS

Listed below are relative comparisons of the skill levels required for installation of various flooring materials. Consider your proficiency when deciding whether to contract a job or do it yourself.

Solid and manufactured wood	Basic woodworking.
Resilient and laminate flooring	Installing tiles is easy. Sheet goods require accurate measuring and cutting and help with handling.
Ceramic tile and stone	These require precise layout and placement and special tools for cutting.
Carpet	Requires special tools, accurate cutting and seaming, and help with handling.

PLANNING

Whether or not you install the flooring yourself, you'll want to do a certain amount of detailed planning to ensure that the finished job looks and lasts exactly as you expect it to. Planning starts with measuring the room and making a drawing showing the shape and dimensions of the floor. This drawing serves two purposes:

■ Dealers and installers can use it to estimate or bid materials and labor costs.

■ You can compute areas and plan the layout of your materials with the drawing. It will also remind you of any quirks in the room that

you should plan for if you lay the flooring yourself. The drawing begins with a sketch.

SKETCHING THE ROOM

Rooms come in an infinite variety of shapes and sizes. Some consist of four straight walls, others have nooks, jogs, and crannies, built-in closets, cabinets, and appliances. When you make your dimensioned drawing, measure everything—exactly. First, make a rough sketch of the contours of the room, identifying appliances, closets, cabinets, doorways, and built-in furnishings.

Then start in a corner and measure the length of every surface to the point where it changes direction. Include the depth of toe-kicks under appliances, cabinets, and other built-in furnishings, and don't forget the area covered by things you will move out of the way, such as the refrigerator. Record the measurements on your sketch. The illustration on the opposite page shows how to check the room for square and curved or bowed walls. Don't be surprised if the room isn't square and regular—rooms seldom are. However, there are ways to accommodate irregularities.

Now transfer your sketch and all of its details to graph paper. Use a scale that is comfortable (¼ inch=1 foot is convenient). Be sure to transfer all of the measurements and irregularities noted on your sketch to the graph paper. If you're planning to install different materials in different rooms, note where each one starts and stops. When you're done, your drawing will look something like the one at left. Now you're ready to make material estimates and move on to some more detailed planning activities.

SCRAPS AND SURPLUS

Even if you plan carefully, you're bound to have material left over. Save it for later repairs.

Resilient and ceramic materials patch easily; repairs cost far less than installing new material. Besides, saved scrap will keep you from having to remember the name of the pattern when a repair is needed. Carpet patches are almost invisible if the materials match. Save some in a dark room and some in a lighted room so you can get the best match if light has changed the color of the carpet on your floor.

MAKING ESTIMATES

Somewhere on your dimensioned plan, compute the total area of each room that will have a new floor. Rooms with four walls and no built-in furnishings or appliances are easy. Simply multiply the length by the width.

ROUGH MATERIAL ESTIMATES
LR: 18 × 17 = 306 sq ft ÷ 18 (strip or bundle coverage) + 10% = 19 Bundles
DR: 14 × 13 = 182 sq ft ÷ 25 (number of tiles/box) + 10% = 8 Boxes of parquet tile
Kitchen: 9 × 8 = 72 sq ft ÷ 1¹⁄₁₂ (area of 1 tile w/grout) = 67 (number of tiles) ÷ 28 (number of tiles/box) + 10% = 3 boxes of ceramic tile
Family room: 23 x 14 = 322 sq ft ÷ 9 = 35.7 sq yd = 36 sq yd +20% = 43.2 sq yd of carpet

In rooms with nooks, crannies, and closets, you will have to compute the area in smaller sections, then add the results to get the total. You may find it easiest in some rooms to multiply the largest dimensions, then subtract the area occupied by permanent features. Don't forget to include the areas under toe-kicks in your totals.

The information in the charts below and on the following page will help you find reliable estimates for costs of materials and supplies. It will also help you prepare preliminary sketches for laying out the materials. Charts on subsequent pages will help you estimate hardwood materials and grout quantities for tile.

CHANGING YOUR MIND

Now is the time to experiment with patterns and layouts. Pattern choices for solid and manufactured wood are fairly limited—they're almost always installed parallel to the long wall in a room. The same is true for

CHECKING THE ROOM FOR SQUARE

1. Snap chalk lines at midpoints of walls.

4 feet 5 feet 3 feet

2. Measure 3 feet exactly on one line, 4 feet on the other. If distance between points is 5 feet, the room is square.

3. Adjust lines until distance is 5 feet.

4 feet 4 feet, 11¾ inches 3 feet

Cut flooring along irregular walls to fit contour.

HOW MATERIALS ARE SOLD

Estimating material quantities is not as exacting as people often assume. All you need to know is how materials are sold and the area of your floor. Then add an allowance for doorways, seams, errors, and waste. The information below will get you started.

Flooring material	Sold by:
Solid wood strips and planks	Sq. ft. in bundles. An 8-ft. nested bundle covers 18 sq. ft. Add 8 to 10 percent.
Manufactured flooring	Sq. ft. Packaging varies by manufacturer.
Tile (parquet, resilient ceramic and dimensioned stone)	Sq. ft. in boxes. Add 8 to 10 percent. The area a box will cover varies with material and style.
Resilient sheet and carpet	Sq. yd. in rolls, commonly 12 ft. wide. Add 4 ft. to each dimension for cutting, 8 to 10 percent for seams and 20 percent for pattern matching.
Laminates	Sq. ft. in cartons. Add 8 to 10 percent. The area of coverage varies with manufacturer and style.

unpatterned carpet, although with any carpet you want the seams to go where the traffic is least. Parquet, resilient, and ceramic tile offer many design possibilities. Experiment on tracing paper laid over your graph paper so you can make changes without erasing and starting over.

DESIGN TOOLS

Your home center may carry design kits that include graphic representations of furniture, appliances, and other decorating features. These kits have stick-on or magnetic profiles of furnishings to help you plan everything to scale. Design programs for home computers are also available from software outlets.

IT'S THE LAST THING YOU DO

Installing a new floor is actually one of the last steps in remodeling a room. If you're planning to paint or wallpaper, do it before tackling any of the floor work. It's a lot easier to clean up the old floor than it is to try to protect your new floor from potential damages from other remodeling projects.

PLANNING

continued

LAYOUT METHODS

SOLID WOOD, MANUFACTURED, AND LAMINATE FLOORING

4 ft. | 5 ft.

Layout lines

Starting line snapped at each wall

3 ft.

Reference lines

Chalk line adjusted for square

TILE (PARQUET, RESILIENT, AND CERAMIC)

Start tile installation here

4 ft. | 5 ft.

Chalk line adjusted for square

3 ft.

(Optional: tack 2×2 battens along layout lines)

PERIMETER ALTERNATE FOR TILE OR BORDERS

Chalk line adjusted for square

4 ft. | 5 ft.

3 ft.

Width of parquet or resilient tile, or width of ceramic tile including grout

ESTIMATING HARDWOOD STRIP FLOORING

(Board feet, assuming 5 percent waste)

Area sq. ft.	Flooring size, inches						
	¾×1½	¾×2¼	¾×3¼	½×1½	½×2	⅜×1½	⅜×2
5	8	7	6	7	7	7	7
10	16	14	13	14	13	14	13
20	31	28	26	28	26	28	26
30	47	42	39	42	39	42	39
40	62	55	52	55	52	55	52
50	78	69	65	69	65	69	65
60	93	83	77	83	78	83	78
70	109	97	90	97	91	97	91
80	124	111	103	111	104	111	104
90	140	125	116	125	117	125	117
100	155	138	129	138	130	138	130

GETTING IT RIGHT

Your new floor will look just right if you align patterns, grout lines, wood grain, carpet pile, and other repetitive features of the material. In other words, the layout of the materials can make or break your design. You'll physically lay out the materials after you have prepared the subfloor, but using layout techniques in the planning stages will keep any mistakes on paper, where they are easy to correct.

LAYOUT METHODS

There are three general methods for laying out a floor. Which one you use depends largely on the flooring material you've chosen. Wood strips and planks almost always begin along or close to one wall. So does carpet. Parquet and other tiles generally start in the center so the materials along the edges can be cut evenly.

All layout methods, however, begin with reference lines at a true right angle at or near the center of the room. Use the 3-4-5 triangle (see page 35) to establish reference lines, and adjust one or both of them until the angle is exactly 90 degrees. Then follow the directions below and in the illustration above left when establishing layout lines. Transfer them to your dimensioned drawing when necessary.

STARTER LINE METHOD: This works for wood strip and plank floors without a border. Establish a starter line at one end of the room by marking the floor an equal distance at each end of your reference line. Tack or chalk a line between your marks and align the first course of flooring on it.

QUADRANT METHOD: Parquet and tile can be laid out this way. The quadrant method makes it possible to create a symmetrical layout in any room (no matter how out-of-square it is) and to finish the installation at opposite walls with cut tiles of equal size.

You begin using this method by establishing the center point. Mark the midpoints of all four walls. Snap a chalk line between each pair of opposite midpoints. If the two chalk lines are not exactly perpendicular to each other, adjust one or the other until they are (use the 3-4-5 triangle). Lay down a trial run of tile in both directions and adjust tiles until borders are even. Begin the installation of each quadrant at the intersection.

PERIMETER METHOD: Lay out bordered floors and some tiled installations this way. Measure from both reference lines toward the wall a distance that equals the full tile (or board) width, plus any allowance for expansion space, grout lines, or irregularities in the wall.

Whatever method you use, test it on paper to see what the final layout will look like before you install the flooring. Consider especially the placement of cut material when installing piece goods, such as tile. Don't lay small pieces of flooring at the edges of the room or across high-traffic areas because they do not look as good or wear as well there as larger pieces.

ESTIMATING ERRORS

Estimating tile quantities isn't always a straightforward mathematical problem. For some materials and styles, the mathematical method of computing room area and dividing it by the amount of coverage in a package of tile will work just fine. In other cases, it will deceive you. For an example, take a look at the layout at top right.

The area of this floor is 79 square feet (182×62 = 11,284÷144 = 78.36). You might believe from that calculation that you would need only seventy-nine 12-inch-square tiles to cover it.

If you purchased cartons of 25 tiles, each of which covered 26.5 square feet (allowing for spacing between tiles), you could assume that 3 boxes, totalling 79.5 sq. ft., would do the job. However, these computations do not take appearance into account.

Edge tiles in a layout should not be less than half the width of a full tile. The layout shows tiles 2 inches wide along two edges.

To fix that, on the graph paper layout remove the 2-inch edge tiles plus one full adjacent tile along the edges. That leaves an uncovered area 14 inches wide along the edges, shown in the middle drawing. Next, shift the remaining full tiles to the center of the layout so the borders will be an even 7 inches all around. Draw in the new edge tiles. You'll find that you need 56 full tiles plus 40 more for the edges—a total of 96 tiles, or four boxes (which will give you four spare tiles).

ESTIMATING GROUT SQ. FT. PER LB.

Tile Size	Joint width, inches					
	1/16	1/8	1/4	3/8	1/2	3/4
1"×1"×1/4"	5.0	2.5	1.0	–	–	–
2"×2"×1/4"	10.0	5.0	2.0	–	–	–
4¼"×4¼"×5/16"	14.5	7.0	3.0	–	–	–
6"×6"×1/4"	25.0	12.0	5.0	3.5	2.4	–
6"×6"×1/2"	12.5	6.0	2.5	1.7	1.2	–
4"×8"×1/2"	11.0	5.5	2.2	1.5	1.0	–
8"×8"×1/4"	33.0	17.0	6.6	4.5	3.0	2.4
8"×8"×3/8"	22.5	11.5	4.5	3.0	2.0	1.6
8"×8"×3/4"	11.0	5.5	2.7	1.5	1.0	0.8
12"×12"×3/8"	28.0	14.0	7.0	4.5	–	2.0
12"×12"×3/4"	14.0	17.0	7.0	–	–	1.0
16"×16"×3/8"	45.0	22.5	9.0	5.7	3.7	3,0
24"×24"×3/8"	65.0	32.5	13.0	9.0	6.0	4.8

ESTIMATING TILE

Preliminary Layout (79 tiles)   15 full tiles+2-in. cut tile=182 in.

2-in. cut tiles

62 in.

182 in.

7-in. cut tiles

Revised Layout (with tiles removed to allow borders to be at least half a tile wide)   5 full tiles+2 in. cut tile=62 in.

Final Layout (with more than half tiles on all borders= 96 tiles)

8½ in.

8¾ in.

8½ in.

9 in.

When working with tile layouts and estimates, always be sure to include the grout size as part of the area covered by the tile.

GROUT WIDTH

An 8½-in. tile with ¼-in. grout line covers an 8¾-in. square.

An 8½-in. tile with ½-in. grout line covers a 9-in. square.

UNDER THE FLOORING

Before you decide on the covering for your finished floor, take a look at what's underneath it. The flooring material you're going to install is essentially a skin over the structural floor that holds up everything (the walls, furnishings, and occupants) and keeps out moisture and drafts.

Familiarizing yourself with the construction of your floor system can keep you from covering up problems that will affect both the materials you've chosen and their installation. It will also save you from undoing mistakes.

Most houses are built with either a wood frame or a concrete slab structural floor, and, in one way or another, both rest on a foundation wall or footings.

WOOD FRAME FLOORS

The primary structure of a wood frame floor is a system of *joists*, generally 2× stock set on edge on 16-inch centers and supported by either foundation walls, bearing walls, or piers, posts, and girders. At the perimeter, a girder or rim joist ties them together. Perpendicular or angled *bridging* adds strength along the joists and prevents them from twisting or bowing under the load above.

The joists are covered with a *subfloor* (generally plywood, structural composition board, dimensional lumber, or tongue-and-groove planks) that distributes weight evenly over the joists and provides a stable surface for the finished flooring.

Next comes the *underlayment*, which adds rigidity to the finished floor, increases its resilience, provides a smooth surface for the flooring material, and protects it from moisture, drafts, and dust below. Although some materials can be laid directly over a subfloor, most materials require some kind of underlayment sandwiched between the subfloor and the finished materials.

The kind of underlayment depends on the type of finished floor materials (see illustration below). Padded carpet may not require an underlayment at all, but other materials call for plywood (from ¼ inch to ¾ inch thick, either sanded or unsanded). Floating floors need a foam underlayment made specifically for this kind of installation. Ceramic tile requires cement backerboard.

SLAB FLOORS

A slab floor is a continuous thickness of concrete spanning foundation walls or footings (often poured as one unit). The thickness of the slab depends on the structural requirements of the building. From the ground up, slab construction starts with a moisture barrier that covers the soil and keeps ground moisture from migrating up into the

ANATOMY OF A WOOD FRAME FLOOR

Stud

Ceramic tile with adhesive

Hardwood with felt paper

Carpet with pad

Resilients with adhesive

Sill plate

Backerboard

Subfloor

Band joist

Mud sill

Foundation wall

Moisture barrier over soil in crawlspace

Bridging

Plywood underlayment

Header

Girder

Joists

Pier and post

ANATOMY OF A CONCRETE SLAB FLOOR

Adhesive · Ceramic tile · Waterproofing membrane · Resilient sheet or tile · Adhesive · Moisture barrier · Mud sill · Stud · Carpet · Pad · Hardwood · Felt paper · Foam pad · Moisture barrier · Reinforcing mesh · Concrete footing with rebar (not found on above-grade slabs) · Slab below grade · Gravel base · Moisture barrier on top of gravel base

concrete and flooring. A bed of gravel (or sand and gravel) supports the slab and minimizes cracking. The slab is reinforced with wire mesh. Underlayments are required for nailed materials and floating floors installed over concrete slabs, but are not always needed for glued-down materials.

TROUBLE UNDERNEATH?

A knowledge of your flooring construction will allow you to troubleshoot it before you install your finished floor. The essential question is: Is the existing subfloor in good enough condition for new flooring?

You can get a pretty good idea of the condition of your floor by removing a floor vent. At a minimum, you can see the number of flooring layers already installed. If you have several, it's best to remove them. Here are some other clues to look for:

WOOD FRAME FLOOR:
■ **SAGGING/SPLIT JOISTS** will cause uneven flooring surfaces and can even split and crack your new flooring. (See page 87 for a remedy.)
■ **SQUEAKS AND NOISES** are an indication of subfloor problems. (See page 87 for solutions.)
■ **SETTLING FOUNDATIONS** make floors uneven and can result in severe damage. The only adequate repair is to jack up the house and reinforce or reinstall the foundation.
■ **MOISTURE** in a crawlspace can ruin the floor above it. (See page 87 for solutions to moisture problems.)

CONCRETE SLAB:
■ **MOISTURE** is the worst enemy of floors on slabs, and it's one that comes with the territory. Concrete retains a certain amount of moisture for months after it's poured and it's not waterproof. It will wick moisture from the ground and the surrounding air. Check for moisture and eliminate it before laying your new floor. (See pages 46–47.)
■ **CRACKS** can mean serious structural problems (sinking floor, footings, or foundation walls) or may require only minor repairs. Consult an engineer or contractor if you don't know what's causing the problem. At worst, you may have to pull up the old slab and pour a new one (or sections of it). If the situation is less serious, you may be able to treat it as a surface problem. (See pages 46–47.)
■ **CHIPS AND SURFACE BLEMISHES** aren't a major problem, but they need to be patched before installing the finished floor. (See pages 46–47 for solutions.)

UNDERLAYMENT

Underlayment has more than one meaning. It usually refers to nonstructural material (plywood, foam, or oriented strand board) that is added just before the finish floor is installed.

However, it also describes any layer immediately below the finished floor—even the subfloor itself or an existing floor that will function as a base for your new flooring. When ordering materials or discussing your floor with a professional, make sure you are talking about the same thing.

GETTING THE ROOM READY

REMOVING BASEBOARDS

Cut paint line with utility knife.

Pull baseboard away with pry bar.

Scrap wood

WOOD BASEBOARDS

Pull nails from back with nippers.

Preparing your floor for its new covering means removing things—baseboards, moldings, and the existing flooring. Of course, not all new flooring will require removal of the existing floor—some can be laid over the old floor. Charts at the beginning of each of the next chapters will tell you whether you need to take up the old flooring for your installation; if you do, follow the steps below.

Leave the doors hanging for the time being, unless you need to remove them to take up the old flooring. With the doors in place and the subfloor exposed, you can easily trim the doors so they will clear the new underlayment and flooring. Remove the doors if you're sure they will swing over the new flooring.

EDGES FIRST

Take off the shoe moldings and baseboards or the cove moldings first. Before you start to remove them, cut along the paint line at the top of the base molding with a knife. This will keep you from pulling the paint off the wall when you remove the molding.

SHOE MOLDINGS: Start removing shoe moldings in one corner. Some corners are coped, with one piece cut to fit against the face of the other. For those, slide a thin putty knife behind the corner of the cut piece, and work it out until you can get a pry bar behind it. Pry against a piece of scrap wood so you don't dent the baseboard.

Work the nail out carefully—you may have to partly remove the next nail to avoid splitting the wood. Repeat the process for all the nails in that section. Number the pieces if you're going to reuse the shoe molding; they won't go back in a different order.

BASEBOARDS: After you've cut the paint line, use the same procedures you employed to remove the shoe molding—

PREPARATION SEQUENCE

Regardless of whether the floor is wood frame or slab, your preparation will be more efficient if you organize your efforts.
- Remove appliances and floor-mounted fixtures.
- Remove baseboards and shoe moldings.
- Put an exhaust fan in a window to increase ventilation.
- Paint or put up new wallcoverings.
- Cover openings with plastic sheets.
- Cover heat and return air ducts.

VINYL COVE BASE

Pull base away with putty knife.

Remove adhesive residue.

Cut paint line with utility knife.

CERAMIC TILE

Pop tiles with pry bar and remove adhesive residue.

SAFETY FIRST

Preparing an old floor is demolition work—and it's not without its dangers. Always:
- Wear boots and work gloves.
- Wear a dust mask or respirator.
- Wear knee pads—kneeling on nails, splinters, and broken ceramic tile can cause serious injuries.
- Don't remove any existing resilient flooring without determining whether it contains asbestos. Asbestos fibers (usually found in resilient floors laid before 1986) are dangerous when inhaled. It's safer to cover an asbestos-containing floor with underlayment than it is to remove it.

slide a putty knife behind the board and pull it away with a pry bar. Protect the wall with thin scrap wood and number the pieces if you're going to reuse them. To avoid damaging the face of the baseboard, pull the nails from the back with nippers.

VINYL COVE MOLDING: After scoring the paint line, slide a putty knife behind the molding and strip it off, working as much as possible with the putty knife handle parallel to the floor. Scrape adhesive from the wall.

CERAMIC TILE: Score the joint between the tiles and the wall as described above, then gently tap the end of a pry bar into the joint. When the pry bar can grip the rear of the tile, pop it loose. Protect the wall with a piece of scrap wood.

REMOVE THE THRESHOLDS

Thresholds generally come up easily. If a threshold fits under the door trim, cut it in half with a backsaw first. If it is nailed in place, pry it up with a pry bar, protecting the adjoining floor with a wide-blade putty knife under the bar. If it's fastened with screws, remove them and slide out the threshold.

REMOVING SOLID WOOD FLOORING

You can pry up nailed-down solid wood flooring (both strip and plank) with a pry bar, but you will probably have to cut pieces out to give yourself some working room. Refer to the illustration at right, and cut the flooring as shown. Then, along the length of the board and at each nail, insert your pry bar under the body of the flooring—not under the tongue—and force it up. If you are removing plugged planks, first bore out the plugs, then take out the screws and proceed as above. Pry up boards that are face-nailed.

To remove parquet, force a wide chisel under each piece and tap it loose. Scrape up the adhesive residue.

REMOVING SOLID WOOD FLOORING

TONGUE AND GROOVE FLOORING

1. Make several plunge cuts in one board to the depth of the flooring. Chisel out the cut wood.

2. Use a pry bar to lift the board where it is blind-nailed.

REMOVING WOOD THRESHOLDS

Cut threshold with a backsaw.

Chisel out each piece.

PLUGGED PLANK FLOORING

1. Remove plugs with a plug cutter.

2. Remove screws.

3. Make plunge cuts in one plank as shown for tongue- and groove flooring.

4. Pry up flooring at face nails.

Plug

Screw

GETTING THE ROOM READY
continued

REMOVING RESILIENT SHEET AND TILE FLOORING

1. Cut sheet flooring into 6- to 12-inch strips with a utility knife.

2. Pull up as much as you can by hand.

3. Scrape stubborn pieces and adhesive residue with a floor scraper.

2. Scrape adhesive residue.

1. Pry up tiles with a floor scraper, heating stubborn tiles with a hair dryer.

REMOVING RESILIENT FLOORING

Before removing resilient flooring, check with a professional to make sure it doesn't contain asbestos. Used as a binder in resilient materials installed before 1986, asbestos fibers are harmful when inhaled, and cutting or breaking the flooring will release the fibers into the air.

If your floor contains asbestos, cover it with underlayment and install the new material over it. If it doesn't contain asbestos, use the techniques below to remove it. To make the job easier, rent a floor-stripping machine.

PERIMETER-BONDED SHEET FLOORING: Sheet material stapled or bonded to the floor only at its perimeter pries up easily. Just lift the staples or loosen the bond with a wide-blade putty knife. Then roll the sheet up and take it out of the room. If the piece is large and unwieldy, cut it into strips of manageable sizes. Scrape off the remaining adhesive with a floor scraper.

SURFACE-BONDED SHEET FLOORING: First, use a utility knife to cut the flooring into 8- to 12-inch strips. Then roll the strips off the floor, working the adhesive loose behind the roll with a wide-blade putty knife.

If the flooring has a felt backing, spray it with a water/dish-soap solution to loosen it.

If the flooring is unbacked, have a helper work ahead of you, softening the adhesive with a heat gun (not a torch) as you go. Scrape off the remaining adhesive.

RESILIENT TILE: Soften the adhesive under each tile with a heat gun; starting at a corner, pry up the tile with a wide-blade putty knife. Scrape off the remaining adhesive.

STUBBORN STUFF: If the flooring does not come up easily, you still have another option—remove it along with the underlayment. Set your circular saw to the depth of the underlayment (don't cut into the subfloor) and cut in 4×4-foot sections. Use an old or carbide-tipped flooring blade—sawing through nails will be unavoidable. Pry up each section with a pry bar.

REMOVING CERAMIC TILE

The method you use for taking up ceramic tile will depend on whether it has been set with a thinset mortar or in a mortar bed. Be especially careful next to floor drains. Wear safety goggles when breaking and removing ceramic tile.

THINSET INSTALLATIONS: To remove thinset tile, chip out the grout around one tile with a hand maul and cold chisel. Then break the tile with the maul and take out the pieces. Hold the cold chisel under the edge of each tile and pop them loose with a sharp tap of the maul.

MORTAR-BED INSTALLATIONS: It's often easier to remove the mortar bed in sections rather than trying to remove individual tiles. First, break the bed into manageable sections by striking the corners of the tiles with a large sledge hammer. Work from the center of the bed to the perimeter. Then insert a large wrecking bar under one corner of the mortar bed (you may have to take up a tile or two to give yourself more working room). Pry up the sections until you can get a wire snips into the joint to cut the reinforcing mesh. Remove each section and haul it out of your way.

REMOVING CARPET

Conventional and cushion-backed carpet are installed differently and require different removal methods.

CONVENTIONAL CARPET: First, remove all the metal edgings. Then cut the carpet into 12- to 18-inch sections with a utility knife. Pry up one corner with a screwdriver and pull it away from the tackless strip on adjacent walls. Roll up each strip and dispose of it. If the carpet is tacked, remove a few tacks and pull the carpet up. If that doesn't work, you'll have to pry up each tack individually.

Tear up as much of the pad as you can by hand and pull the staples with a cat's paw. Then pry up the tackless strips with a pry bar.

CUSHION-BACKED CARPET: Cut the carpet into 12-inch strips with a utility knife. Pull up each strip, working it free as you roll

REMOVING CERAMIC TILE

1. Score the first tile with a chisel and small sledge, then break out pieces.

2. Tap a masonry chisel under an adjacent tile and pop it free.

3. Chip out grout as you go.

it back. Drive a wide-blade putty knife between the backing and the floor to break the adhesive bond. Scrape up the remaining adhesive and chunks of cushion backing with a floor scraper or wide chisel.

REMOVING CARPET

CONVENTIONAL CARPET

1. Cut carpet at threshold with utility knife.

2. Cut carpet into 12-inch strips

3. Pull carpet from tackless strip and roll it up.

4. Remove staples with nippers.

CUSHION-BACKED CARPET

1. Cut carpet into 12- to 18-inch strips and roll it up.

2. Scrape cushion residue and adhesive with a floor scraper.

PREPARING A WOOD SUBFLOOR

Most of the preparation for wood subfloors consists of making surface repairs and installing underlayments. Subfloor defects will be magnified by the layers you put on top, so be sure to make all surface repairs to the subfloor before you lay down underlayment or new flooring.

First, inventory the problems. Look for high spots, low spots, protruding nails, gaps, chipped-out areas, and other defects.

MARKING THE DEFECTS

Divide the floor into imaginary 6-foot sections and, within each section, rotate a 6-foot level. Mark all defects with a carpenter's pencil. Drive in any protruding nails, then turn to the remaining problems in the following order:

CHECKING THE SURFACE

Rotate a 6-foot level across sections of the floor. Mark areas that need repair.

Low area, chip

High spot

PREPARING THE SURFACE

Level high spots with a belt sander, fill dents and low spots with filler and smooth, and reset protruding nails.

FIXING SAGS AND QUIETING SQUEAKS

Drive shim between joist and subfloor.

Fasten loose flooring with screws from below.

Wedge a 2×4 cleat snugly to the subfloor and screw it to the joist.

SAGS AND SQUEAKS

A sagging floor means that a joist is sagging, either due to failure of its support or because of warpage. Floor squeaks occur when something moves or rubs—the finish floor moving against the subfloor, for instance.

FIXING SAGS: Refer to the illustration above. There are two ways to stabilize the subfloor—you can either attach a cleat to an existing joist, or drive shims between the joist and the subfloor. Choose the method that best fits the situation, and follow the directions in the illustration.

QUIETING SQUEAKS: Squeaks may be caused by nails that have worked loose or boards that have shrunk or cupped. Anchor the loose flooring with 6d or 8d ringshank nails driven at an angle. If the squeak persists, drill pilot holes and countersink wood screws through the floor into the joists.

CRACKS, CHIPS, AND DENTS

If your new flooring calls for plywood underlayment, you can skip some subfloor repairs. However, if your new flooring requires an absolutely smooth surface—cushion-backed carpet or resilient materials, for example—you may have to repair chips and dents in the underlayment itself.

To fill depressions, choose a filler that is compatible with any sealers or adhesives you plan to use later. Most fillers are water- or latex-based. First vacuum the area, then mix the filler just before you use it—fillers set up quickly. Trowel it into the depression and feather the edges with a wide-blade putty knife while it's still pliable. After it's dry, sand it flush with the surrounding floor.

HIGH SPOTS AND SLICK SURFACES

Use a belt sander to level out any high spots and warped boards you have marked. If a board is badly warped, remove that section from joist to joist. If your new flooring requires adhesive and the subfloor is slick, roughen the surface with a medium-grit sandpaper attached to a long-handled block.

UNDERLAYMENTS

Different flooring materials call for different kinds of underlayment. Refer to the illustration on page 38, and install the underlayment best suited to your new flooring. For more information, refer to the chapter in this book that covers your particular type of new flooring.

PLYWOOD: This sheet material is made of an odd number of thin wood layers glued under pressure with the grains of each layer at right angles to the others. Plywood won't warp, buckle, twist, cup, or split. Install underlayment-grade plywood. Sold in a range of grades, thicknesses, and sheet sizes, its smooth outer face satisfies the general subsurface requirements of most finished floors.

TILE BACKING UNITS: Fiberglass-and-concrete backerboard is designed to underlay ceramic and dimensioned stone tile. Unlike plywood, it provides no structural strength and must be installed over a subfloor. It can be used in both dry and moisture-prone areas.

LIQUIDS: Liquid underlayments are used to smooth, level, fill, patch, and even moisture-proof subfloors. Most should be applied by professionals.

TRIMMING DOORS AND CASINGS

To trim a door so it clears your new flooring, lay a piece of the flooring material on the underlayment and mark the door at a point ⅛ to ⅜ inch higher. Remove the door as shown in the

illustration, center right. If a nail won't work, try tapping a screwdriver blade under the edge of the hinge pin or remove the hinges from the door. Trim the door as shown. Cut the door trim to the thickness of the new flooring with a trim saw.

INSTALLING PLYWOOD UNDERLAYMENT

Joints staggered every 4 ft.

⅛-inch expansion gap

¾-inch plywood

Fasteners 6 inches on center on perimeter

Plank subfloor

Joist

Fasteners 10 inches on center

8d nail used for spacing

16d nail in joist

8d ringshank nails

TRIMMING A DOOR

Mark door ⅛ to ⅜ in. higher than the new flooring.

Remove bottom hinge pin first, then others, and pull door away.

Score trim line with a utility knife and cut with a circular saw.

Mask cut line on both sides to prevent door from splintering.

TRIMMING THE DOOR CASING

Use flooring thickness (including underlayment) to mark and cut stops and casing.

Door casing

Stop

Trim saw

PREPARING A SLAB

All flooring materials must be installed over a dry surface. And although preparing a concrete slab for new flooring involves many of the same steps required for a wood frame floor, concrete brings with it additional concerns because of its ability to absorb moisture. Correct the moisture problems first.

will collect in the surrounding soil and migrate into the slab. These and several other problems are fairly easy to correct. The illustration below shows typical solutions.

Moisture wicking up from the soil is more difficult to correct. Unless a moisture barrier was laid over the soil before a below-grade or on-grade slab was poured, the slab may wick up moisture from the ground. Tracking down and correcting moisture problems caused by wicking may require professional help.

WET SLABS— CAUSES AND CURES

Several factors contribute to moisture problems in slabs. Missing or inadequate gutters and downspouts or soil that drains toward the foundation will let water in. Without a subsurface drainage system, water

CHECKING FOR MOISTURE

Alkali deposits on the slab, or damp, puffy-looking, or buckled flooring are danger signals. To check for moisture, tape 2×2-foot clear plastic squares to the floor every 2 feet. After a couple of days, lift them. If droplets have formed under the plastic, or the plastic looks cloudy, you probably have a moisture problem.

SURFACE REPAIRS

After correcting moisture problems, check your slab's surface with a 6-foot level, and mark any defects.

CRACKS AND HOLES: Key minor cracks or holes with a chisel, clean them out, and fill them with a quick-setting hydraulic cement. Major cracks may be a sign of structural failure. Consult a pro for recommendations.

LOWS AND HIGHS: Fill depressions with patching compound, feathering it to the surrounding floor. Grind high spots down with a rented concrete grinder. If extensive leveling and smoothing are both required, consider using a liquid underlayment.

ALKALINE SALT DEPOSITS: Alkaline deposits will interfere with adhesive bonding on glued-down floors. Remove them by mopping the surface with a solution of 4 parts water and 1 part muriatic acid. Then rinse the slab with clean water. Muriatic acid is hazardous; follow directions carefully.

SOLVING MOISTURE PROBLEMS

Preventing Condensation

1

2

Fiberglass between 2×4 studs

1. Vent cool air to outside.
2. Extruded polystyrene fastened with masonry fasteners.
3. Slope soil away from house.
4. Waterproof membrane extends 3 inches above soil.

Install gutters, downspouts, and extensions.

3

Exterior Drainage System

4

Fine sand or pea gravel

Extruded polystyrene

Sump connected to drain pipe

Coarse gravel

Interior Drainage System

Remove concrete and replace after installing drain pipe.

Plywood over insulated slab

Sump connected to drain pipe

Coarse gravel

Seal block cores.

Bricks

Dimpled sheeting covers walls and floors.

Insulated frame wall

Venting Crawlspaces

Vent crawlspaces every 4 feet and cover soil with 6-mil polyethelene.

MAKING SURFACE REPAIRS

Key minor cracks (enlarge them at the back) and fill with hydraulic cement.

Break out damaged areas and fill low spots.

Level high spots with a carbide grinder wheel.

Roughen surface if necessary.

ROUGH AND CLEAN IT

Adhesives will not bond to slick or dirty surfaces. Break the sheen caused by sealers (if water sprinkled on the slab beads, the slab has been sealed), paint, or a steel-trowel finish by sanding the concrete lightly with a medium-grit abrasive on a long-handled wood block. Scarify hard surfaces with a rented scarifier. Then scrub the slab with a degreasing agent or a trisodium phosphate solution and hot water. Rinse with clean water and let dry.

INSTALLING SLEEPERS

Solid wood floors and other nail-down flooring require a wood surface to drive nails into. You can fasten plywood underlayment directly to a slab or you can install it over wooden sleepers, as shown at right.

Either installation will support any material that can be laid on plywood underlayment. Even though you can install most glue-down and floating floors directly on a slab, sleepers will insulate the flooring from the cold concrete and help make the finished surface more comfortable.

To install sleepers, first vacuum the slab and seal it with asphalt primer. Then spread a ⅛- to ¼-inch layer of asphalt mastic over the entire floor. Lay a moisture barrier over that. On 16-inch chalk lines, embed pressure-treated 2×4s in a mastic bed and anchor them with concrete nails. Leave a gap between the sleepers for circulation. Cover the sleepers with ⅝ or ¾-inch plywood. Cut out 2×8-inch holes every 6 feet along the walls perpendicular to the sleepers, to allow air to circulate under the floor. Insert floor grilles after you have installed the finished floor.

INSTALLING A SLEEPER SUBFLOOR

Fasteners every 6 inches on perimeter, 10 inches within sheet

½-in. gap at walls

½-in. gap at walls

Polyethylene moisture barrier overlapped every 6 inches (or asphalt sealer)

Vent for circulation

¾-in. plywood

Pressure-treated 2×4 sleepers spaced 16 in. OC

½-in. gap between sleepers

1½-in. foam insulation (optional)

Masonry fasteners

Mastic bed   Mastic

INSTALLING WOOD FLOORS

Wood flooring will give years of service when installed over a subfloor that is structurally sound, dry, relatively level, smooth, and free of dust and foreign matter. The chart on the opposite page shows how to prepare a floor for new wood flooring.

Installation of all solid wood products is fairly straightforward, once you have established your layout on paper and transferred it to the floor. The illustration on page 50 will help you plan the installation if your project involves more than one room.

When you're satisfied that the subfloor is ready and the layout is just the way you want it, you're ready to bring in the materials.

Hammer

Chisel

Framing square

Jigsaw

Drill and bits

Miter box

Blind nailer

Because damp air makes wood swell and dry air makes it shrink, you'll have to protect your materials from extremes of temperature and humidity.

To keep the wood dry and ready for installation, don't have it delivered during rain or snow. For new construction, don't deliver the flooring until after the building is enclosed and all the concrete work, plaster work, and painting are finished and completely dried.

Acclimate the wood in the room where it will be installed, at a temperature of 65 to 70 degrees. Stack the material log-cabin style—or just spread it around the room—for at least five days before you install it.

ORIENTATION

Strip, plank, and manufactured flooring are normally laid perpendicular to the floor joists and parallel to the long wall in the room. If you run the flooring parallel to the joists, you must install at least two layers of ¼-inch plywood and strengthen the floor with additional bridging (every 2 feet) between the joists. Parquet pieces are usually square, so joist direction is not relevant.

To determine the joist direction and position, look at the nails on the subfloor (or look from below if the subfloor is covered). Mark the center of each joist on the walls, so you can see the marks when you're nailing.

PREPARING A FLOOR FOR WOOD FLOORING

Find your existing floor in the left column below, then prepare the floor as shown.

Existing Floor	T&G or Square-Edge	Parquet or Glue-Down	Floating Floor
Exposed joists	1. Install ¼-inch plywood. 2. Lay felt paper.	Install ¼-inch plywood.	1. Install ¼-inch plywood. 2. Install foam underlayment.
Bare concrete	1. Install sleepers or ¼-inch plywood subfloor. 2. Lay felt paper.	1. Remove sealer/finishes. 2. Repair and roughen surface.	1. Repair surface. 2. Install foam underlayment.
Wood subfloor or finish floor over wood frame or concrete slab	1. Repair surface, install ¼-inch plywood as needed. 2. Lay felt paper.	Remove finish, repair surface. On rough surface or planks wider than 4 inches, install ⅜- or ½-inch underlayment.	1. Repair surface. 2. Install foam underlayment.
Resilient sheet/tile	If existing resilient is cushioned or loose, remove and repair surface. Otherwise, repair surface.	If existing resilient is cushioned or loose, remove and repair surface. Otherwise, repair surface.	If existing resilient is cushioned or loose, remove and repair surface. Otherwise, repair surface.
over wood frame	1. Install ¼-inch underlayment-grade plywood. 2. Lay felt paper.	Install ⅜-inch underlayment.	Install foam underlayment as needed.
over concrete slab	1. Install sleepers or ¼-inch plywood subfloor. 2. Lay felt paper.	1. Remove wax or finish and roughen surface. 2. Lay felt paper.	Install foam underlayment.
Ceramic tile	Remove tile and repair surface.	If tile is bonded, remove finish, level, and roughen surface. Otherwise, remove tile,	
over wood frame	1. Install ¼-inch plywood as needed. 2. Lay felt paper.	repair surface, and install ⅜-inch underlayment.	1. If tile is bonded, remove finish and level surface. 2. Install foam underlayment.
over concrete slab	1. Install sleepers or ¼-in. plywood. 2. Lay felt paper.	Repair surface as needed.	Same as above.
Carpet			
over wood frame	1. Remove carpet and pad. 2. Repair subfloor as necessary. 3. Install ¼-inch plywood as needed. 4. Lay felt paper.	1. Remove carpet and pad. 2. Repair subfloor.	1. Remove carpet and pad. 2. Repair subfloor. 3. Install foam underlayment.
over concrete slab	1. Remove carpet and pad. 2. Install sleepers or ¼-inch plywood. 3. Lay felt paper.	1. Remove carpet and pad. 2. Repair surface. 3. Remove sealer/finish and roughen surface.	1. Remove carpet and pad. 2. Repair surface. 3. Install foam underlayment.

INSTALLING TONGUE-AND-GROOVE FLOORING

PLANNING THE LAYOUT FOR MULTIPLE ROOMS

4. Keep going.

6. Reverse orientation with spline (see page 52).

5. Keep going.

1. Mark perpendicular reference lines.

3. Lay floor in this direction.

2. Measure equal distance at both ends and establish starter line.

7. Continue to wall.

Strong, interlocking tongue-and-groove joints create a surface that functions as a single unit. Before laying tongue-and-groove flooring, install felt paper as an underlayment. This will cushion the flooring and keep noise down by preventing the wooden surfaces from touching when they flex.

LAYING THE FELT

Follow these steps to install the felt underlayment.
- Mark the joist locations. Make the marks on the wall.
- Lay down strips of 15-pound asphalt felt paper perpendicular to the new flooring. Overlap all edges 4 inches and trim the ends so they lie flat.
- Staple or tack the felt paper across its surface and at the edges; countersink the fasteners slightly. Then, from one wall to the other, snap chalk lines on the felt paper at the joist marks.
- Establish the starting wall. It's usually best for your starting wall to be opposite a doorway. At each end of the starting wall and ¾ inch out from it (to allow for expansion), measure from your reference line and tack a nail at both points. Stretch a line between the nails—this is your layout line. If the starting wall is not square with the rest of the room, use the quadrant layout method (see page 36). This will ensure that the floor looks square, because the flooring will be in line with the centerline of the room.

TONGUE-AND-GROOVE NAILING SCHEDULE

This chart shows the nail sizes and spacing for blind-nailed T&G flooring.

Flooring in Inches	Barbed Fastener Size	Spacing
⅜×1½	1¼-in. machine-driven fastener; 4d screw, cut steel, or wire casing nail	8 in.
½×1½	1½-in. machine-driven fastener; 5d bright wire casing nail	10 in.
¾×1½	2-in. machine-driven fastener; 7d or 8d screw or cut nail	10–12 in.
¾×2¼	2-in. machine-driven fastener; 7d or 8d screw or cut nail	10–12 in.
¾×3¼	2-in. machine-driven fastener; 7d or 8d screw or cut nail	10–12 in.
¾×3 to 8	2-in. machine-driven fastener; plank 7d or 8d screw or cut nail into and between joists	7-8 in.

For ½-in. plywood subfloor, fasten at and between each joist.

On slab with ¾-in. plywood, use 1½-in. fasteners.

THE STARTER COURSE

The starter board should always be your longest, straightest board.
- Lay the starter board—tongue toward the center of the room—against the starter line with its end ½ inch from the side wall. Mark joist locations on the face of the board closest to the wall and predrill at the marks at the proper interval for your flooring (see Nailing Schedule at left).
- Lay the board exactly on the starter line, then face-nail and countersink the board with the fasteners specified in the nailing schedule.
- At the same locations on the tongue, predrill holes at a 45-degree angle and blind-nail the tongue by hand. Drive nails partway and countersink the heads with a nail set, being careful not to mar the face or tongue.
- Cut a board to fit the remainder of the wall and install it in the same fashion.

RACKING THE FIELD

To ensure a random joint pattern, loosely arrange the next seven or eight courses, mixing long and short lengths from different bundles. Overlap the joints by at least 6 inches. If you're laying planks of various widths, make piles of each width and rack from each pile so you won't run out of a width before finishing the room. Plan each course to start with the piece left over from the previous one if it's at least 2 feet long.

INSTALLING SOLID WOOD FLOORS

LAYING THE FIELD

Begin each course at the same side wall, and leave ½ inch at the ends. Snug each board into place with scrap flooring and blind-nail the tongues by hand. When you have enough room to get behind a power nailer, finish the remainder of the floor, keeping your toes on the previous strip or plank. Rack several courses and start nailing 2 inches from the end of each board. Drive at least 2 nails in each board, no matter what its length. When you come across a bent board, refer to the illustration at right.

LAYING FELT PAPER

Mark joist locations on walls.

Snap chalk lines on felt paper at joist marks for nailing guide.

Overlap felt paper by 4 in.

Staple felt paper to subfloor.

1. Lay the first seven or eight courses loosely, staggering the joints by at least 6 inches.

Snug hand-nailed courses with scrap flooring.

2. Face-nail the first board and blind-nail by hand until you have room to use the nailing machine.

45°

Face-nail first board in predrilled holes.

Set nail with nail set.

Scrap flooring

Wood block

USING BENT BOARDS

1. Tack a wood block to the floor with duplex nails.

2. Force the warped board in place with a crowbar.

3. Keeping pressure on, drive duplex nails into scrap to hold flooring until you can nail it.

TONGUE-AND-GROOVE FLOORING
continued

MEETING OBSTACLES

If the starting wall has a doorway, you will need to change the direction of the tongue edge so you can continue blind-nailing the boards through the doorway. Glue a spline into the groove of the nearest board. Then install the reversed courses.

If the floor has furnace vent holes or other obstructions, cut and fit the flooring around them, mitering corners where possible. Rip off the exposed tongue on a table saw.

REVERSING DIRECTIONS

Spline glued to both grooves.

FRAMING OBSTACLES

Crosscut flooring to fit the length of vent openings.

THE LAST COURSES

As you approach the opposite wall and run out of room for the power nailer, blind-nail the tongues by hand. When you don't have room to swing the hammer for blind-nailing, face-nail the boards. Scribe the final course to the contour of the wall if necessary (leave a ¾-inch gap). Pull it into place with a pry bar leveraged against scrap on the wall, as shown below. Face-nail the final board.

INSTALLING TRANSITIONS

Wood threshold

Reducer strip

FINISHING UP

Where the two floors are of different heights, a reducer strip will ease the transition. Where the heights are the same, install a tapered threshold. Nail the baseboards at the studs and angle-nail the shoe molding to the baseboard, not to the flooring, so the flooring can expand and contract freely.

Fill unfinished face-nailed flooring with a wood filler, or prefinished flooring with a color-matched putty stick. Next, sand and seal unfinished floors (see pages 88–89). Clean and buff prefinished flooring.

THE LAST COURSE

Scrap wood

¾ inch

1. Rip the last board to fit between flooring and wall.

Outside corner (miter cut)

INSTALLING BASEBOARDS

Baseboard

Shoe molding

Stud

Molding

Subfloor

Inside corner (coped cut)

INSTALLING SQUARE-EDGE FLOORING

Installation of square-edged flooring begins with felt paper underlayment (see page 50) and calls for the same basic techniques as tongue-and-groove flooring. Instead of blind-nailing, however, each board is fastened with face-nails. The work will go faster if you rent a nail gun that countersinks the nails when it drives them.

BORDERING A FLOOR

If you plan to install a border, refer to page 37 for information about perimeter layouts. Establish a starter line on each wall, each line ¾ inch away from the wall and square with the other lines. Then select your first board and predrill holes 1 inch from each end and at 7-inch intervals along the board, as shown below right.

Keeping the edge of the plank on the line, face-nail it as shown in the nailing schedule at right. Finish the first course to the end of the wall. Follow the sequence shown and complete the border, measuring each course exactly so it butts tightly. Snug each board along its length with a chisel leveraged into the floor. Then lay the field.

THE SQUARE-EDGED FIELD

Dry-lay the field, rack it (see page 51), and face-nail the field. Predrill the holes if necessary and keep each board snugly against the previous one.

PLUGGING PLANKS

Plugged fastener holes lend a rustic touch to planked flooring, but they require a little forethought. First, measure and mark each plug location—about 1 inch from each end. A 3-inch plank gets 1 plug, a 5-inch plank gets 2, and a 7-inch plank, 3. If you're using preplugged planks, duplicate and mark the plug pattern on the ends of any boards you've cut. Predrill holes at the marks and follow the directions in the illustration below to set them.

SEQUENCE FOR INSTALLING A BORDER

NAILING SCHEDULE FOR SQUARE-EDGE FLOORING

This chart shows the nail sizes and spacing for square-edged flooring.

Flooring in Inches	Barbed Fastener Size	Spacing
$5/16 \times 1\frac{1}{4}$	1-in. 15-gauge fully barbed flooring brad	5 in. on alternate sides
$5/16 \times 1\frac{1}{2}$	1-in. 15-gauge fully barbed flooring brad	2 nails every 7 in.
$5/16 \times 2$	1-in. 15-gauge fully barbed flooring brad	2 nails every 7 in.

7 in.   7 in.   1 in.

1. Predrill holes 1 inch from ends, then every 7 inches along the board.

2. Using techniques for tongue-and-groove flooring, rack the floor, lay the first plank on the starter line, and face-nail it with floor brads.

3. Lever the boards in place by digging a chisel into the subfloor.

SETTING PLUGS IN PLANKS

With random-width planks, use cut-off pieces to begin rows of the same width.

Counterbore holes.

Tighten screws.

Chisel and sand level with floor.

INSTALLING MANUFACTURED WOOD FLOORING

Manufactured flooring is made for today's do-it-yourself consumers. While installation of solid wood requires some carpentry skills and is time-consuming, manufactured flooring can be installed relatively quickly and doesn't call for special skills.

Most products are designed for either glue-down or floating installations, but a few are made for nailing. (Some products are made for installation by any of the three methods.) Be sure to follow the manufacturer's installation recommendations.

If your flooring is designed for nailing, employ the procedure described on pages 50–52 for tongue-and-groove flooring. If your material is designed to be glued or floated, follow the instructions on these two pages. Regardless of the method, when you cut the material, refer to the illustrations on the opposite page so the pieces will fit and won't have frayed edges.

TROWELS AND ADHESIVES

Manufactured wood flooring is made to precise tolerances and specifications, and each product will carry with it specific recommendations for fasteners or adhesives and spreading trowels.

Be sure to follow the recommendations. Don't assume that an adhesive that worked well for your parquet or resilient tile will suit your new wood floor. Using products or tools not recommended by the maker could result in a voided warranty.

LET IT ACCLIMATE

Manufactured flooring is a wood product, and like solid wood flooring, it must be acclimated to your house before you install it. If you're laying the floor in a newly constructed or remodeled room, give any plaster, drywall compound, concrete, or latex-based paints plenty of time to dry to make sure the room is dry. After you prepare the subfloor, unpack the flooring in the room and let it sit in its new environment for at least five days.

INSTALLING A GLUE-DOWN FLOOR

Fit edges together and butt ends snugly.

Glue ends of planks as recommended by the manufacturer.

Tap each plank into place snugly with a piece of scrap flooring.

Use a pull bar (or pry bar and scrap) at walls to pull flooring into place.

INSTALLING A FLOATING FLOOR

1. Roll out underlayment and dry-lay the first course against ½-inch spacers.

½-inch spacers

3. Snug each glued board into place with scrap flooring.

Scrap flooring

4. At the wall, use a pull or pry bar to pull the course tight.

2. Lift the first board and apply glue according to the manufacturer's directions.

5. Continue dry-laying two courses at a time, gluing and snugging flooring together.

INSTALLING A GLUE-DOWN FLOOR

Prepare the surface and lay underlayment as recommended on page 45.
■ To give yourself some working room, lay out the floor with the starter line (see page 50) about 3 feet from one wall.
■ Dry-lay and rack several rows (some products are preracked). Spread adhesive on only as much area as you can cover within the adhesive's open time. Spread adhesive along the layout line, but don't cover the line.
■ Glue the ends (not the sides) of the first board and install it with the tongue to the wall, leaving a ½-inch expansion gap at the end. Angle the tongues of successive courses into the grooves of the preceding ones and slide the end joints together immediately.
■ Cinch the flooring tight every several courses by tapping boards with a hammer and scrap piece. Pull the ends tight at the wall with a pry bar or flooring tool as shown above.
■ When you reach the wall, go back and lay in the bare floor that was your working room when you started the installation.
■ Roll the entire floor with a roller.

FLOATING A FLOOR

Lay a floated floor over a foam underlayment recommended by the manufacturer. Prepare the floor, then:
■ Snap a starter line ½ inch from the wall or dry-lay the first boards against spacers. Trim the board as needed, and apply glue according to the manufacturer's recommendations. (Some recommend putting it on the tongue, some in the groove, some on both.)
■ Dry-lay several courses to establish the recommended pattern. Follow the procedures shown above to lay the rest of the floor.

6. At final course, hold template plank securely against wall and mark final course for cutting. Cut and install.

Scrap flooring

Template plank
Mark cut line on this board.

CUTTING MANUFACTURED WOOD FLOORING

Face down

Face up

Face up

Face down

INSTALLING WOODBLOCK AND PARQUET FLOORING

PARQUET AND WOODBLOCK LAYOUT

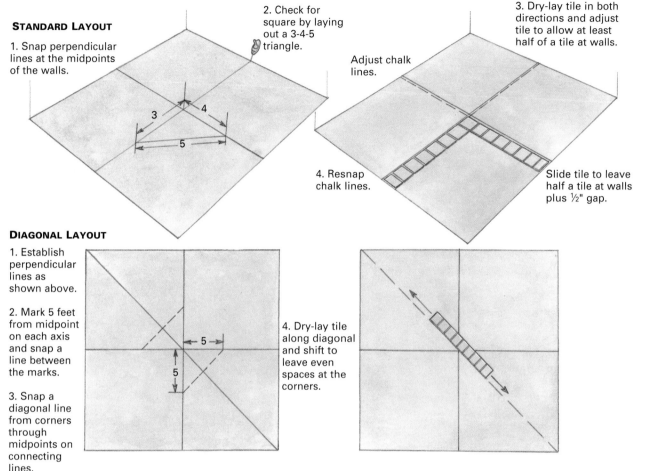

STANDARD LAYOUT

1. Snap perpendicular lines at the midpoints of the walls.

2. Check for square by laying out a 3-4-5 triangle.

3. Dry-lay tile in both directions and adjust tile to allow at least half of a tile at walls.

Adjust chalk lines.

4. Resnap chalk lines.

Slide tile to leave half a tile at walls plus ½" gap.

DIAGONAL LAYOUT

1. Establish perpendicular lines as shown above.

2. Mark 5 feet from midpoint on each axis and snap a line between the marks.

3. Snap a diagonal line from corners through midpoints on connecting lines.

4. Dry-lay tile along diagonal and shift to leave even spaces at the corners.

Parquet flooring comes in the form of square tiles, so the floor usually looks best if you lay it out to make the borders even on all walls—except those with doorways. As with other tile installations, the quadrant layout method works well (see page 36 and the illustrations above). Prepare the floor, then vacuum it before snapping layout lines. If you clean it after you lay it out, you'll remove the chalk lines.

LAYING OUT THE FLOOR

Using the information on page 36 and the illustration above, snap a chalk line at the center of the room. Snap a second line at the middle of the first one and perpendicular to it. Establish a 3-4-5 triangle to adjust the line square with the first.

Diagonal patterns require another set of squared lines, as shown above. Establish one diagonal using the method shown. Make the second diagonal perpendicular to the first so the lines are square to each other.

THE TEST RUN

Lay a dry run along both layout lines until you get the pattern centered in the room. Begin the test layout at the quadrant with a doorway. Lay a row of blocks from the center point toward the doorway wall and slide the row back and forth until you have a full block at the doorway, less ¼ inch for expansion. Snap a new line where the center-most block now falls; repeat the process on the other axis, sliding the tiles until the borders on both ends are equal. Then bring the parquet cartons into the room and put them around the room so you can reach them easily.

SETTING THE FIRST QUADRANT

Pros say applying adhesive is "all in the wrist" (and, of course, to some extent in the manufacturer's recommendations).
■ Dump or scoop a small amount of adhesive on the floor and—holding a toothed trowel at a 35- to 45-degree angle—spread enough

adhesive for six to eight blocks. Don't cover the chalk lines. If you do, snap lines over the adhesive.

■ Set the first tile in the adhesive exactly at the intersection of the layout lines. If this tile is positioned incorrectly, everything else will be —and the error will be compounded across the room. Insert the tongue of each tile into the groove of the previous tile, and press each one tightly into place by hand. (Refer to the illustration at right.) Don't slide the tiles into place—adhesive will ooze through the joint. Clean adhesive off the surface immediately.

■ Fill the quadrant according to the pattern sequence you have chosen, working toward the walls.

■ At the walls, use the process illustrated below right for marking and cutting border tiles to fit. For complex shapes, cut an exact template from cardboard and trace it onto the wood block to serve as a guide. Cut the blocks with a fine-toothed backsaw or saber saw when you need to fit them around obstacles.

■ As you run out of room to work freely and need to walk or kneel on the tile, lay down plywood to distribute your weight and to avoid displacing or scuffing your new floor.

■ Fill the expansion gap with cork to keep the tiles from shifting.

SEQUENCE FOR LAYING TILE

Chalk lines

Spread your weight evenly on a 2×2' plywood sheet.

■ Follow the same process to install the other quadrants. When you're done, don't walk on the floor yet. Let it stand as long as the adhesive manufacturer specifies. Then finish it if necessary, and trim and rehang the doors. If the parquet is prefinished, clean and buff it.

INSTALLING PARQUET TILE

1. Apply adhesive with a notched trowel up to but not covering the layout line.

2. Lay the first tile exactly on the layout line.

Layout line

3. Engage tongues and grooves of succeeding tiles and lower into place. Don't slide them.

4. At walls, lay the tile to be cut squarely on the last full tile and use an extra tile to mark the cut.

Tile to be cut

Spare tile used as marking guide

½- to ¾-in. spacer

PAINTING A FLOOR

Painted floors, whether they are wood or concrete, bring a special touch to any room. Paint is durable, attractive, and reasonably priced. It's an easy project for the do-it-yourselfer and offers endless opportunities for artistic expression.

The range of styles and techniques is limitless. The four techniques shown here are within the skills of any homeowner.

WHAT TO PAINT ON?

Any stripped wood floor, wood subfloor, or concrete slab can be painted. Paint may not stick well to resilient tile, resilient sheet, or ceramic tile, so it's better to remove those materials. The surface must be smooth and clean, so prepare it as you would for installing resilient flooring. Vacuum the floor and wipe it with a tack rag. Then seal it and paint it with one coat of high-quality, oil-based, exterior-grade primer.

WHAT KIND OF PAINT?

There are two basic paint choices—oil-base or latex. Special floor paints are available.

■ Oil-base paints create a hard film and cover a poorly prepared surface better.

■ Latex paints will give you a more resilient film and, because they breathe, are more suitable in damp environments such as basements or concrete slabs.

STENCILING

Lift stencil while paint is wet and move to next frame.

Reference lines

Stencil taped in place

Surface sanded, cleaned, primed, and sealed.

■ Alkyd or modified epoxy latex porch and floor paints dry to a durable surface, but color selection is limited.

■ Industrial enamels are tough, but their high gloss tends to make them slippery.

■ Porcelain-epoxy paints are excellent. Some lighter colors come in a satin finish.

SEAL THE FLOOR

Sealer closes pores in the wood and leaves a smooth base for the remaining coats. Test the drying time on scrap wood, then apply the sealer as recommended by the manufacturer. Wipe the excess after 10 minutes, and buff it with steel wool when dry. Then dust with a tack rag.

STENCILING

If you want wood tones and grains to show through your pattern, stencil right over the sealed floor. Otherwise, prime and paint the surface with two coats of oil or latex paint. Map out your design layout and snap perpendicular lines at both the center of the room and at locations that will keep the pattern regular and square. Tape the stencil into place and apply paint with a stencil brush. Lift the stencil before the paint dries. Wait 24 hours and apply a polyurethane finish.

COMB PAINTING

Comb painting is a repeated pattern of swirled lines made with a window squeegee you've cut notches into or other notched tool.

COMB PAINTING

Surface prepared and painted with oil-base paint.

Notched window squeegee

Wet top coat

Grid lines

Comb top coat while it's still wet.

Prime and paint the floor with two coats of light-colored oil-base paint. Then tape a grid on the floor in 12- to 24-inch sections. Thin a contrasting color with one part thinner to three parts paint and paint a section with this mixture. While this coat is still wet, run your comb through it to create patterns. When the design coat is dry, pull the tape up to reveal the colored borders.

MARBLEIZING

Marbleizing requires patience and practice. Experiment on a piece of plywood first.
■ Prime and paint the floor with two coats of semigloss latex. Then set out three pie tins—these will be your palettes.
■ In tin No. 1, thin some white latex paint and tint it with another color to a light neutral tone. In tin No. 2 put thinned white paint and at each edge dab different, brightly colored acrylics. Create veins in this tin by dragging the acrylics into the white paint

MARBLEIZING

Brush first coat from tin No. 1.

Sponge second coat from tin No. 2.

Add veins from tin No. 3 with artist's brush.

Tin No. 1 — Thinned white latex, tinted to neutral tone.

Tin No. 2 — Thinned white latex veined with acrylics.

Tin No. 3 — Dabs of unthinned acrylics.

with a sponge applicator. In tin No. 3 put dabs of unthinned acrylic colors.
■ Brush paint from tin No. 1 on the floor to create a neutral base. Immediately sponge with a paint pad containing the veining from tin No. 2. Add more veins from tin No. 3 with an artist's brush.

SPATTER PAINTING

Prime and paint the floor with two coats of floor enamel. When it's dry, spatter on another color. To spatter, load the brush with paint, then flick the brush to fling paint spots onto the floor. Repeat with a third color.

SPATTER PAINTING

Spatter succeeding colors after each coat has dried.

Surface prepared, primed, then painted with a solid color.

PAINTING A SLAB

You can dress up a drab slab with paint by using the same techniques used on wood floors. But concrete takes a little more preparation. Here's what you should do:
■ Make sure the slab is clean and dry. If it's new, cure it for at least 30 days before painting. If it's old, test for moisture (see page 46) and correct any problems.
■ Patch cracks and uneven joints with an expansive mortar designed for such applications. Allow it to cure, following the manufacturer's instructions.
■ Scrape off loose or flaking paint, and if the entire old paint job is rough, remove all of it by scraping or stripping it.
■ Scrub the floor with trisodium phosphate (TSP) mixed with water, according to instructions.
■ Etch the concrete with a solution of 1 part muriatic acid in 10 parts water. If you'll be using water-based paint, use phosphoric acid in the same ratio. Be careful; acids are corrosive. Mix them in a plastic pail. Wear rubber gloves and goggles, and follow all precautions on the container.
■ When the floor is dry, vacuum up the dusty residue.
■ Seal the floor (not necessary with an acrylic latex paint or an alkyd porch and floor enamel). Once the concrete is prepared, apply the paint with the same methods used on wood.

INSTALLING RESILIENT AND LAMINATE FLOORS

Sheet vinyl is easy to install, but calls for careful measuring and cutting.

TOOLS FOR INSTALLING RESILIENT FLOORING

Utility knife

Shears

Notched trowel

Chalk line

Tape measure

Stapler

Both resilient and laminate flooring need to be acclimated before you install them. Store materials away from freezing or fluctuating temperatures. Let sheet flooring relax to remove the curl. Unroll it in a room at 70 degrees for 24 to 48 hours before installation. Let resilient tile and laminate boards and planks adjust to their new conditions for at least 48 hours in their unopened containers.

Resilient flooring is the thinnest of all flooring materials, so it will conform to almost every defect in the surface under it—cracks, voids,

dips—even small depressions from nailheads will show. If the subfloor or the existing floor is not smooth, cover it with underlayment-grade plywood to make it smooth.

The subsurface must be absolutely dry too. Unlike wood or carpet, through which small amounts of subsurface moisture can evaporate harmlessly, a resilient floor will trap moisture underneath it. Trapped moisture can weaken the adhesive bond. In humid climates, add a waterproof underlayment material.

PREPARING A FLOOR FOR RESILIENTS AND LAMINATES

CAUTION: Old resilient tile may contain asbestos fibers, which are harmful if inhaled. Covering this old tile with new flooring minimizes its potential hazard. If tile must be removed, consult an asbestos abatement professional.

Existing Floor	Preparation for Resilients	Preparation for Laminates
Exposed joists	1. Install ¼-inch T&G plywood or OSB subfloor. 2. Install lauan plywood or ¼- to ½-inch rated underlayment. 3. Fill all nail holes and joints and sand smooth.	1. Install ¾-inch plywood. 2. Install foam underlayment.
Bare concrete	Level and smooth slab as necessary.	1. Repair surface. 2. Install foam underlayment.
Wood floor or subfloor		
Over wood frame	1. Replace broken floor or subfloor boards. 2. Install lauan plywood or ¼- to ½-inch rated underlayment. 3. Fill all nail holes and joints and sand smooth.	1. Repair surface. 2. Install foam underlayment.
Over concrete slab	1. Remove all wood materials. 2. Level and smooth slab as necessary.	1. Repair surface. 2. Install foam underlayment.
Resilient sheet or tile		
Over wood frame	1. If existing resilient is cushioned, remove and repair surface. If existing resilient is loose, has wax/gloss surface, or is embossed, install lauan or ¼- to ½-inch rated underlayment. 2. Fill all nail holes and joints and sand smooth.	If loose, remove and repair surface. Otherwise, repair surface. Install foam underlayment.
Over concrete slab	If existing resilient is cushioned or loose, remove and level slab as necessary. If existing resilient is embossed, smooth the surface with a liquid leveler; otherwise, remove wax and sand smooth.	Install foam underlayment.
Ceramic tile		
Over wood frame	Remove tile or smooth with liquid leveler. 1. If tile is removed, repair subfloor as necessary. 2. Install lauan plywood or ¼- to ½-inch rated underlayment. 3. Fill all nail holes and joints and sand smooth.	1. If tile is bonded, level surface. 2. Install foam underlayment.
Over concrete slab	1. Remove tile; otherwise, smooth with liquid leveler. 2. If removing tile, repair slab as necessary; if slab is uneven, smooth with liquid leveler.	Same as over wood frame.
Carpet		
Over wood frame	1. Remove carpet. 2. Repair subfloor as necessary. 3. Install lauan plywood or ¼- to ½-inch rated underlayment. 4. Fill all nail holes and joints and sand smooth.	1. Remove carpet and pad. 2. Repair subfloor. 3. Install foam underlayment.
Over concrete slab	1. Remove carpet and pad. 2. After removing carpet, repair slab as necessary; if slab is uneven, smooth with liquid leveler.	1. Remove carpet and pad. 2. Repair surface. 3. Install foam underlayment.

Pry bar

Framing square

Floor roller

Metal straightedge

Handsaw

INSTALLING RESILIENT SHEET FLOORING

Next to proper surface preparation, measuring and cutting are the keys to success when installing resilient sheet flooring. Careful work will save you from wasting the entire sheet.

There are two kinds of sheet flooring: one kind is installed by spreading adhesive only on the edges, the other kind requires spreading adhesive on the entire floor. Cutting both kinds to size and seaming them call for the same techniques.

No matter which style you have, the first thing to do is prepare the surface as outlined in the chart on page 61. Then follow the steps below to make a paper template, a room-sized form that will allow you to fit the sheet exactly to the walls and fixtures of your room.

MAKING A TEMPLATE

Making a template may seem like more trouble than simply bringing the sheet into the room and cutting it. Properly prepared, however, a template will give you a guide for cutting the flooring to fit exactly—without waste or risk of ruining the material.

To make the template, cover the perimeter of the floor with 15-pound felt, other building paper, or heavy butcher's paper, as shown on the opposite page. The heavier felt or building paper is less likely to move around.

■ Position the paper within ¼ inch of the walls, cabinet bases, and other obstacles. The template doesn't have to fit precisely; baseboards and shoe moldings will cover up the difference.

■ To keep the paper from shifting, cut out small triangles every 2 or 3 feet and tape the sheet to the floor underlayment through the holes. Overlap all edges at least 2 inches, and tape them together with a heavy tape such as duct tape.

■ Now that the template is in place, mark a line on the underlayment around the perimeter of the template, using a marker and steel straightedge. When you cut the resilient sheet and bring it into the room, this line will place it exactly where the template was. Then carefully roll up the template and take it to the room where you'll cut the sheet.

TRIMMING THE SHEET

Unroll the sheet flooring face up, if you haven't already done so. If the sheet will be seamed, make sure the pieces overlap by 3 inches at the seam and that pattern lines run unbroken along the length of the seam. Tape the seam securely—don't let it move.

■ Orient the sheet the same way it will be installed in the room, then unroll the paper

TIPS FOR SEAMS

Find the best location for seams before you get the resilient sheet in the room. Pick an inconspicuous, low-traffic area and mark the location of the seam on both sections of the sheet.

RESILIENT FLOORING ADHESIVES

What kind of adhesive should you use for your new resilient floor? It depends on the flooring material and the subfloor. Here are various adhesives and their applications. Always work in a well-ventilated room and follow manufacturer's instructions.

Flooring Material	Subfloor	Adhesive	Comments
Vinyl materials with rubber backing, cork, vinyl cork (not solid vinyl, asphalt, vinyl composition)	Concrete or wood above grade	Water-soluble paste	Must be rolled.
Asphalt, vinyl-composition	Concrete or wood above, on, or below grade	Asphalt emulsion, cut-back asphalt	Do not thin with water for on- or below-grade floors.
Solid vinyl, vinyl-composition, rubber, cork, linoleum	Concrete or wood above, on, or below grade	Latex adhesive	Good for moist locations; dries quickly. Keep from freezing.
Vinyl, rubber, cork, linoleum	Concrete or wood above grade	Alcohol-resin	Flammable. Not entirely waterproof.
Solid vinyl, rubber tiles	Concrete or wood above, on, or below grade	Epoxy cement	Good for perimeter and seam sealing; high strength; two parts must be mixed.
Vinyl and rubber cove base	Above grade	Cove base cement (solvent based)	Flammable; wear gloves.
Vinyl cove base, metal nosings (not asphalt, vinyl composition)	Any wall and edges	Synthetic rubber cement	Flammable.
Vinyl and rubber stair treads, nosings, corner guards	Any wall	Neoprene adhesive	Water resistant. Flammable.

MAKING A PAPER TEMPLATE

Masking tape anchors the template to the subfloor.

Holes

Paper template

Cut into paper to expose subfloor.

Plywood subfloor

Overlap sheets by 2–4 inches and tape ends.

template and position it on the sheet flooring. Line up the edges of the template with pattern lines so the flooring won't look awkward in doorways or along prominent walls. Shift the template on the sheet until it's in the right place.

■ Tape the template to the flooring through the triangular holes—the way you taped it to the underlayment—and trace its edge on the flooring material with a washable marker or, on a glossy surface, a grease pencil.

■ Roll the template up and dispose of it. Holding a straightedge along the marks on the sheet, cut the flooring with a utility knife. Roll up the sheet (don't fold it) with the pattern side in, and carry it to the room.

■ Starting along the wall with the fewest obstacles, unroll the sheet. Slide it under door casings, and tug and shift it into place. Now you're ready to glue it down.

RESILIENT ADHESIVES

The type of adhesive you use will depend both on the type of resilient material you've chosen and the type of subfloor you have. Use only the adhesive recommended by the flooring manufacturer. The most common adhesive, a water-soluble paste, is used on wood floors or slabs above grade.

Asphalt emulsion can be used below grade—it's the one to use for tiling the basement. It is solvent-thinned. Latex formulations and epoxies are also used when water resistance is required.

Some adhesives are flammable, so always be cautious. Ventilate the room and don't use anything that could cause a spark. The chart on the opposite page describes adhesives.

TRIMMING RESILIENT SHEET FLOORING TO FIT

Mark perimeter of template on sheet.

Tape seam securely

Cut away on line around perimeter.

Paper template

3 in.

Overlap seam edges 3 inches

Chalk line marks seam cut.

INSTALLING RESILIENT SHEET FLOORING
continued

ADHERING PERIMETER-BOND VINYL

Perimeter-bond vinyl is glued only around the edges. After you have positioned the sheet in the room, start at a corner and carefully pull back the edge along one wall. Expose about 8 inches of underlayment or subfloor—or as much as the manufacturer recommends.

■ Using a ¼-inch notched trowel, spread a band of adhesive all along the edge of the floor. If the sheet will have a seam in it, stop the adhesive about 18 inches from where the seam edges will meet.

■ Ease the edge of the sheet back onto the adhesive and roll it with a floor roller to ensure good contact. Then move on to the other edges of the floor and finish gluing and rolling each edge in turn.

■ Seam the sheet, following the procedures described on page 65 and illustrated below.

Some products require edge stapling to further secure the sheet to the plywood underlayment. Follow the manufacturer's instructions. Make sure the base trim will cover the staples.

GLUING FULL-SPREAD VINYL

To apply full-spread adhesive, carefully lift up one half of the sheet and fold it back (don't crease it) onto the other half. (See the illustration on the opposite page.)

■ Working from the corners to the center on each length of wall, spread the adhesive on the floor with a ¼-inch notched trowel. Applicators are available for hard-to-reach spots. If the sheet will be seamed, stop the

PERIMETER-BOND VINYL: INSTALLING AND SEAMING

1. Unroll sheet and position it squarely in the room.

2. Fold back the edge at each wall and apply adhesive. Lay the sheet back onto the adhesive and roll.

4. Using a straightedge, cut both pieces with a utility knife.

5. Pull back the sheet at the seam and apply adhesive under it. Push seam edges into adhesive.

3. Remove tape from seam and snap a chalk line at the seam cut.

6. Roll the seam and let the adhesive cure. Then apply seaming solvent.

adhesive about 18 inches short of the seam.

■ Refold the sheet back into place and roll it from the center to the corners. Adhere the second sheet (or the other half if not seaming).

SEAMING SHEET VINYL

Make seams in sheet flooring after the sheets have been adhered.

■ On the face of the seam overlap, snap a chalk line down the center of the seam.

■ Cut with a sharp utility knife against a steel straightedge, with enough pressure to cut through both layers of flooring. Don't cut twice—you'll leave gaps.

■ Remove the scrap overlaps and clean the floor under the seam.

■ Pull back both edges of flooring and spread a band of adhesive along the floor. Join the two edges and press them into the adhesive.

■ Immediately wipe off any adhesive that oozes up between the pieces, and clean the seam with a solvent for the adhesive.

■ After the adhesive has set for the time specified by the manufacturer, seal the seam with seaming solvent, which melts the edges and fuses them to make the seam waterproof. The solvent bottle comes with a special applicator spout which you run along the seam, following the directions on the label. Apply the sealer only to the seam, not to the flooring. To finish the job, replace the trim, install baseboards and shoe molding or vinyl cove base (see illustration below). Install thresholds and rehang the doors.

INSTALLING FULL-SPREAD SHEET VINYL

1. Unroll sheet and position it squarely in the room.

2. Pull back one half of the sheet and apply adhesive to within 18 inches of the seam.

3. Pull back the other half and apply adhesive.

4. Seam the sheet, following the procedures illustrated on the opposite page.

5. Roll the entire surface with a floor roller.

IMMEDIATELY AFTER INSTALLATION

After you've laid your new resilient floor, take these steps to protect it until both adhesive and seams have set.

■ Protect the seams for at least 8 hours. If possible, don't walk on them.

■ Keep the room at 65 degrees or above for 48 hours to let the adhesive cure properly.

■ Don't scrub or wash the floor for 5 days.

INSTALLING VINYL COVE BASE

1. Cut all corners first, scoring the cove base as shown. Apply adhesive to the grooved back of the vinyl only. Warm the vinyl with a hair dryer and roll it into place with a rubber roller.

2. Cut straight pieces and fit between corners.

For an outside corner, warm the vinyl when installing. It will stretch to fit around the corner.

For an inside corner, score the back lightly from top to bottom. Notch the flange to form a corner when folded.

Press flange with scrap wood.

Outside corner

Inside corner

INSTALLING RESILIENT TILE

STANDARD LAYOUT

Snap perpendicular lines at the midpoints of the walls and square them to each other. Dry-lay tile in both directions to center layout. Snap new chalk lines.

DIAGONAL LAYOUT

Lay out perpendicular lines as shown below and snap diagonal lines (see page 56). Dry-lay tile along a diagonal and shift the tiles to leave even spaces at the corners. Snap a perpendicular line at the center of the tile layout.

Just about anyone can install resilient tile. It requires few special tools and the materials are not particularly expensive. If you do make a mistake, you've only lost one tile—and you might be able to use it along an edge.

Prepare the floor using the information on page 61, then sweep and clean it.

LAYOUT

The quadrant layout method (see page 56 and the illustration at left) works best for most tile installations. It allows you to center the pattern with equal-width cut tiles along the edges. For durability and appearance, borders that extend into an opening or a doorway should have full tiles. If the room is irregular or contains many built-in protrusions, mark the reference lines—either square or diagonal—on the largest rectangular portion of the floor.

Next, test the layout. Dry-lay tiles along both axes, starting at the center and working toward the walls. If you end up with less than half a tile at the wall, adjust the test run on that axis until the edge tile is at least a half tile. Continue testing layouts with dry runs until you're satisfied with the way the borders look. Then mark your layout lines again.

SETTING THE FIRST QUADRANT

Before opening the can of adhesive, read the label to find out its open time—how many minutes you have before the adhesive becomes too dry to make a good bond. Some adhesives will allow you enough time to set only six or seven tiles; with others you'll be able to set most of a quadrant.

■ With the smooth side of a notched trowel (use the size recommended by the adhesive

INSTALLING RESILIENT TILE

Lay tile at the edge of layout lines and other tiles, then gently drop it into place.

Spread adhesive up to, but not covering your layout line.

Lay tile according to your layout plan.

manufacturer), spread a small amount of adhesive at the intersection of your layout lines. Don't cover the lines. Avoid spreading it too thick, which will cause it to ooze between the tiles; or too thin, which will not produce a good bond. Then use the notched side of the trowel to comb the adhesive. Allow the adhesive to become slightly tacky before setting the tiles.

■ Carefully position the first tile so it's perfectly aligned on the intersection of both layout lines. Set the next few tiles along each axis. Then fill the area between the axes, working toward the walls.

■ Snap the tiles into place; don't slide them. Work very carefully. Minor errors early can build to major alignment problems later.

■ Continue laying tiles along each axis and filling in the area between them.

■ Cut tiles at the borders and to fit around obstacles as shown in the illustration below. Resilient tiles can be brittle when cold. Warm them briefly with a hair dryer to make the cuts easier.

INSTALLING SELF-STICK TILE

Make cuts before removing backing.

Peel off backing.

Press into place, placing corner of tile next to those already laid.

FINISHING UP

Finish the other three quadrants in the same manner as the first, starting in the center of the room and working out along both axes. To prevent displacement of newly laid tiles, lay a 2×2-foot piece of plywood over tiles before walking or kneeling on them.

Watch for adhesive oozing out of the joints. Wipe it up immediately with a rag and a compatible solvent.

Don't walk on the floor until the adhesive has set. Check the manufacturer's instructions for set-up time. When the floor can safely be walked on, install the finish details.

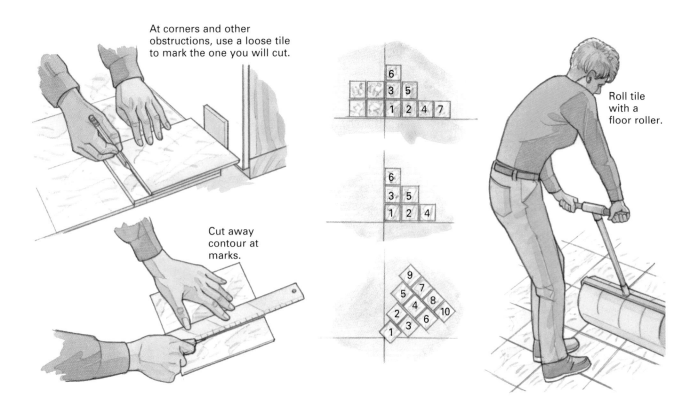

At corners and other obstructions, use a loose tile to mark the one you will cut.

Cut away contour at marks.

Roll tile with a floor roller.

INSTALLING LAMINATE FLOORING

Although laminate flooring needs a smooth and level subfloor, its foam underlayment makes it somewhat forgiving of subfloor imperfections. Manufacturers specify ventilation requirements, so if your floor will be over a crawlspace, make sure it meets the specifications.

Prepare the floor as shown in the chart on page 61, making surface repairs to wood frame floors and slabs as discussed on pages 44 and 45.

UNDERLAYMENT FIRST

After you have properly prepared the subfloor—including laying a vapor barrier over a slab—lay down the underlayment. Start in a corner; butt the end of the underlayment against one wall. Unroll the underlayment to the other wall and

GLUING TIPS

Glue on tongue

Glue in groove

Glue should squeeze slightly out of joint.

Not all brands of laminate flooring are glued the same way. Some manufacturers recommend gluing the tongue of the board, others the groove, and still others, both the tongue and groove. Follow the directions and use only the glue specified by the manufacturer.

One requirement that is consistent among products is the amount of glue to apply—and getting this right might take some experimenting. Properly applied glue should just barely seep from between fully closed joints. If you're applying too little, the boards won't stay together; too much, and you won't get the boards together tightly or you'll have excess glue to clean up.

FLOATING A LAMINATE FLOOR

4. Pull the course tight at the wall with a pull or pry bar.

1. Roll out the underlayment and dry-lay the first course against ½-inch spacers.

½-in. spacer

5. Continue dry-laying two courses at a time, gluing and snugging the flooring together. Pull the flooring snug at the walls with a pull bar.

2. Lift the first board and apply glue according to the manufacturer's directions.

Scrap flooring

3. Snug each glued board into place; protect the edge with scrap flooring.

cut it to fit. If the manufacturer recommends laying a section of flooring at this point, start the next step and rotate through the steps for underlayment and installation. Otherwise, stick with unrolling the underlayment, butting each strip against the previous one (don't overlap them). Tape the seams (unless the manufacturer recommends otherwise). If you're using solid-panel underlayment, use the same methods, but leave a ¼-inch expansion gap between the panels.

THE FIRST PLANK

If your starting wall is square to the room, dry-lay the first row against ½-inch spacers, as shown in the illustration on the opposite page. Or you can use the starter-line layout method shown on page 36. When you get to the side wall, lay a plank next to the first one and mark a cut line. Transfer the line to the back of the plank. Cut the plank with a carbide-tipped blade in your circular saw (turn the plank facedown when cutting). Set the cut board in place and pull it snug with a pull bar or pry bar.

At each end of the first plank and in the middle, measure from the edge to the opposite wall. If the measurement will divide by the plank width and leave more than 2 inches, dry-lay two more rows. If you won't have at least a 2-inch plank on the far wall, split the difference between the first and last rows and trim the first row accordingly. Then continue dry-laying the next two rows, racking the ends if necessary.

Manufacturers' recommendations for the amount of joint overlap differ. Refer to the illustration at right if your flooring does not come with specific instructions.

GLUING THINGS DOWN

Once three courses are laid, you can start gluing. Make sure the courses are running straight in the room. Take up all the planks except the first one—number them or keep them in order—and apply glue to the planks as specified by the manufacturer. Set the planks back in place, press them together, and wipe off excess glue immediately. Tap the blocks together and clamp them as specified by the manufacturer. Continue to dry-lay, glue, and clamp, starting each row with the piece left over from the previous one, if the piece is a foot long or more.

WHAT GOES UNDER THE FLOORING?

Laminate flooring materials require a foam underlayment, which cushions the floor underfoot. Underlayment also deadens sound and allows the entire floor to function as a single unit held down by the base moldings.

Installation on a concrete slab requires a moisture barrier. Some floating-floor manufacturers build a moisture barrier into underlayment. Others require a two-step application. Be sure to use only the materials recommended by the manufacturer of your flooring. Some choices are:

■ **6-MIL POLYETHELYENE:** Keeps moisture out of the laminate flooring, but requires a separate foam underlayment.

■ **2-IN-1 FOAM:** A more expensive product than separate moisture barriers and underlayments, but it allows you to cover the floor in one application. Install the film side down (facing the slab).

■ **FOAM UNDERLAYMENT:** This companion to polyethylene moisture barriers is made of closed-cell poly.

■ **RUBBER-BACKED AND SOLID POLY:** A more expensive product, but worth it if you want the most comfortable floor and the highest degree of sound absorption.

THE FINAL PLANK

Mark the width of the last row and apply glue to the plank. Set it in place with a pull bar, or lever it with a pry bar and a piece of scrap. Remove excess glue, and let the floor set overnight before you walk on it.

Some laminate planks have a soft, almost clear grain with no strip or plank division. Use these layout methods with them.

LAMINATE PLANK PATTERNS

Joints fall on midpoint of previous plank.

Minimum 12-inch stagger

Two-plank stagger

x=stagger width

Laminate planks are also manufactured in two-plank or three-strip configurations, each with racked or staggered joint lines.

Stagger joints 6 to 8 inches

Three-strip stagger

CERAMIC TILE
& DIMENSIONED STONE

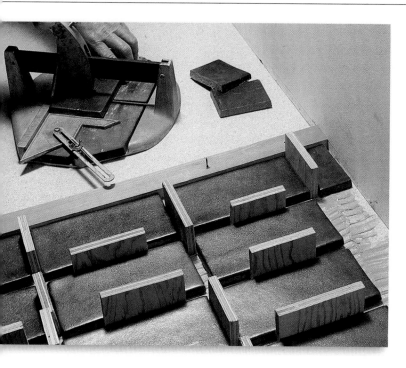

Ceramic and dimensioned stone tile are the heaviest of flooring materials, so they require a floor structure that has been designed or reinforced to carry the weight. If you plan to lay tile over an existing tile floor, remove the existing tile first to reduce the weight.

Ceramic and dimensioned stone tile are the most stable of flooring materials, but like other materials it's better to let them sit in the room before you install them. Bring the materials in one day before installation to equalize the temperature of the tile and the subfloor. Arrange the cartons so you can reach them easily but still keep them out of your way. Store the tiles in a separate room if the subfloor isn't prepared yet.

Cement backer board provides a smooth surface that makes installation of ceramic tile and stone over a wood frame floor easier.

Chalk line

Hammer

Tape measure

Float

Notched trowel

Pry bar

Nippers

Hacksaw with rod blade

Glass and tile cutter

Framing square

Beater block

Snap cutter

Installation on a concrete slab usually requires only surface repairs. The chart at right shows how to prepare your subfloor. Your local rental outlet has special tools that are not normally part of your do-it-yourself tool box.

Procedures for installing either ceramic tile or dimensioned stone tile are similar, but stone tiles come with some of their own peculiarities. You must cut them with a tile-cutting saw; trying to cut stone with nippers or by scoring and snapping usually fractures it. Joints between stone tiles must be tighter than joints for ceramic tiles (usually not more than ⅛ inch), which reduces layout flexibility. The natural grain of the stones that makes cutting difficult also gives each piece a distinctive look.

PREPARING A FLOOR FOR CERAMIC TILE

Exposed Joist	Install a double-wood subfloor—¾-in. T&G CDX plywood on the joists and underlayment-grade plywood or tile-backing units over the subfloor.
Bare Concrete	Make surface repairs to slab as needed. Roughen the surface for best adhesion.
Wood Subfloor Over wood frame	Make surface repairs as needed. Install underlayment-grade plywood or tile-backing units over subfloor.
Over concrete slab	Remove all wood materials to expose the slab. Make surface repairs to slab as needed. Roughen the surface for best adhesion.
Wood Finish Floor Over wood frame	Remove finish flooring to expose the subfloor. Install underlayment-grade plywood.
Over concrete slab	Remove all wood materials to expose the slab. Make surface repairs to slab as needed. Roughen the surface for best adhesion.
Resilient Sheet or Tile Over wood frame	If the resilient flooring is installed over particleboard underlayment, remove both. If the resilient flooring is installed over plywood, is dense (neither cushioned nor springy), and is sound, remove wax or finish. Otherwise remove the flooring to subfloor. Install underlayment-grade plywood or tile-backing units.
Over concrete slab	If the resilient flooring is cushioned, springy, or unsound, remove it and make surface repairs to the slab as needed. Otherwise remove wax or finish and use an adhesive compatible with the resilient flooring.
Ceramic Tile Over wood frame	If possible, remove existing tile, then install underlayment-grade plywood or tile-backing units over the subfloor. Otherwise secure loose tiles and roughen the surface. Smooth uneven surfaces with liquid underlayment. Reinforce floor if necessary.
Over concrete slab	Remove existing tile, if possible. Repair slab surface as necessary. Otherwise secure loose tiles and roughen the surface. Smooth uneven surfaces with liquid underlayment.
Carpet Over wood frame	Remove existing carpet and pad, then install underlayment-grade plywood or tile-backing units.
Over concrete slab	Remove existing carpet and pad, then repair slab surface as necessary.

INSTALLATION TECHNIQUES

WATERPROOFING MEMBRANE

Spacer — Ceramic tile — Adhesive

Cement backerboard

Waterproofing membrane

Membrane adhesive

Subfloor

ISOLATION MEMBRANE

Ceramic tile — Thinset adhesive — Isolation membrane

Membrane adhesive

Wood floor

Concrete slab

Ceramic and stone tiles are not flexible, so they require a more rigid subsurface than other materials. Cement backerboard—a laminated sheet of concrete and fiberglass made specifically to support tile—is the best material to use. Many installations are made with plywood under tile, however. In addition, some situations require extra layers of protection beneath the tiles.

WATERPROOF MEMBRANE: A waterproof membrane stops moisture from seeping up through or down through floors. In wet areas, such as shower floors, install a waterproof membrane over the subfloor and under the cement backerboard. See the illustration at left.

ISOLATION MEMBRANE: An isolation membrane protects tile from excessive movement or different rates of movement in underlying surfaces caused by temperature and humidity changes. If you're tiling over different materials, install an isolation membrane as illustrated at left.

LAYING CEMENT BACKERBOARD

Backerboard comes in a number of sizes, and installing it is much like installing drywall. Purchase the size that will result in the

SIZING THE JOINTS

Here are guidelines to help you decide how wide the joint should be for the particular tile you're setting. You can vary the size to suit your installation, but larger joints are more likely to crack. Irregular tiles usually need large joints.
Glazed tiles—³/₁₆ to ³/₈ in.
Porcelain tiles—⅛ to ¼ in.
Terra-cotta tiles—¾ in.
Cement-bodied tiles—³/₈ to ½ in.
Stone tiles—Up to ⅛ in.

ADHESIVES FOR TILE AND STONE

The type of adhesive you use for your tile or stone floor depends in part on the conditions in which it will be installed. The chart below shows appropriate adhesives for several installation conditions. Consult with your tile dealer to make the selection that best fits your project.

Conditions	Type/Composition	Comments
Adhesives		
Damp areas	Type I mastic (solvent based)	Flammable. Possible lung and skin irritant. Thinset. Ready to use.
Dry areas	Type II mastic (latex based)	Easy cleanup, nonflammable.
Wet areas or over plywood or resilient materials	Epoxy adhesive (2-part epoxy)	Expensive, toxic to skin. Works best at 70 to 85 degrees.
Mortars		
Wet areas or uneven subfloors	Portland cement (portland, sand, water)	For reinforced thick-bed installations. Long-lasting, waterproof, strong.
Over cement backerboard, not over wood or resilient floors	Dry-set mortar (portland, sand, additives, water)	Not water-resistant. Nonflammable, easy cleanup, rigid, impact resistant.
	Latex-portland (portland, sand, liquid latex, water).	More water-resistant than dry-set mortar, easier to work.
Wet areas over concrete or ceramic tile	Epoxy mortar (epoxy resin, hardener, sand, portland cement)	More body and water-resistance than epoxy adhesive. Levels uneven surfaces.

LAYING CEMENT BACKERBOARD

1. With the smooth edge of a trowel, spread enough thinset adhesive for one sheet. Comb the adhesive with the notched edge of the trowel.

2. Lay sheets in place, leaving a ¼-in. gap at the wall and a ⅛-in. gap between sheets. Stagger the joints so the edges fall over joists. Fasten the board with corrosion-resistant screws every 8 inches.

3. Smooth adhesive over the joint to 3 inches wide.

4. Embed fiberglass tape in the joint and smooth out excess adhesive.

5. Spread a thin coat of adhesive and feather the edges of the joint.

least waste and follow the procedures in the illustration above. Once the backerboard is in place, you're ready to lay out the room.

LAYOUT

To lay out your installation, use either the perimeter layout method or the quadrant method. We've shown the quadrant method here, because it will result in evenly spaced borders and cut tiles.

Snap chalk lines in the center of the room and square them with the 3-4-5 triangle method. Then lay tiles and spacers along both axes until you get full tiles at doorways and equal tiles on the borders. If the pattern doesn't fit exactly, you may be able to adjust it by changing the width of your grout lines slightly.

Resnap chalk lines at the new locations, then make a jury stick, as shown in the illustration at right. Lay the jury stick along the walls and use it to mark and snap additional layout lines. Additional layout lines keep the pattern from wandering as you lay the tile.

LAYING OUT A TRIAL RUN

Include spacers between tiles when laying out a dry run of ceramic tile.

MAKING A JURY STICK

Width of tile

Width of grout

INSTALLATION TECHNIQUES
continued

SPREADING TILE ADHESIVE

1. Dump just enough adhesive to cover the area and spread it with the smooth edge of the trowel held at a 30-degree angle

2. Comb adhesive with notched edge at a 45- to 75-degree angle.

Smooth edge down

Notched edge down

WHAT TROWEL TO USE?

Type of Tile	Notch Size and Shape
Mosaics and smaller tiles	$\frac{3}{16} \times \frac{5}{32}$ in. or $\frac{1}{4} \times \frac{1}{16}$ in., V
Wall tiles	$\frac{1}{4} \times \frac{1}{4}$ in., square
Flat-backed floor tiles	$\frac{1}{4} \times \frac{1}{4}$ in., square
Irregular or lug-backed tiles	$\frac{1}{4} \times \frac{3}{8}$ in. or $\frac{1}{2} \times \frac{1}{2}$ in., square
Marble and granite	$\frac{1}{4} \times \frac{1}{4}$ in. or $\frac{1}{4} \times \frac{3}{8}$ in., square

- Use the adhesive and trowel size recommended by the manufacturer.
- Keep your layout lines visible; put adhesive up to them, but not over them.
- Place tiles in the adhesive with a gentle twisting motion—do not slide them.
- Immediately clean adhesive from surfaces.
- To level the tiles, press them into the adhesive with a handmade beater block—a carpet-covered length of 2×4.
- In tight places, back-butter the tile by applying a small amount of adhesive on the back of the tile and spreading it with the notched side of the trowel.
- Lay down plywood to walk on set tiles.

SETTING THE FIRST TILES

Setting tiles is a series of repetitive steps. Go slowly at first—you'll pick up speed and expertise as you work. The illustration below will take you through the steps, but here are some things to keep in mind.

CUTTING TILES

Cutting tiles is usually a snap—although sometimes it may be slightly more difficult.

LAYING CERAMIC TILE

1. Spread adhesive within an arm's reach in sections parallel to layout lines.

2. Twist tile slightly as you press it into adhesive.

Reference lines define sections.

Rubber mallet

4. Set the tiles with a beater block.

Beater block

3. Check sections with a straightedge.

2×2 batten tacked to floor as guide

The illustration below right shows the steps in making a cut. Allow yourself to make some mistakes—that's one of the reasons you should buy extra tile. If the layout is regular and perfectly square, cut several tiles ahead of time. Rent a tile saw if you'll have a lot of cuts. The cost will be worth the time saved.

IN DOUBT ABOUT GROUT?

When you shop for grout, you'll find they all do pretty much the same thing and there's not much difference in the way they look.

Most grouts will work with any residential tile installation, but the most common are cement-based grout (a mixture of portland cement and sand or additives) or latex-portland cement grout (like cement grout, but with latex additives).

Look for hardened polymer-modified grouts. They are more flexible, hold color longer, and are more water-resistant than regular grouts. Colored sealant and caulk make expansion joints that match your grout. Sealants last somewhat longer than caulk, but caulk is easier to apply.

GROUTING

When the adhesive has set for 24 hours, remove the spacers between the tiles and mix the grout to about the consistency of mayonnaise. Mix only as much grout as you can apply during the open, or working, time. Apply the grout as shown below. Here are some other points to keep in mind:

■ Grout that has set cannot be remoistened.
■ Pack the joints tightly.
■ Work the float diagonally across— not parallel to—the tiles.
■ After 10 to 15 minutes, remove the surplus
■ After another 30 minutes, wipe away the grout haze with a nearly dry sponge. Let the grout cure, then install a tile base border.

INSTALLING A TILE BASE BORDER

Cut border tile so grout lines continue up from floor.

Apply adhesive to back of tile.

CUTTING CERAMIC TILE

1. Mark cut line.

2. Score cut line with glass cutter.

3. Snap cut line over dowel.

HOW MUCH IS ENOUGH?

Too thick   Too thin   Proper application

GROUTING TILE

Force grout into joints with a grout float.

Sweep grout across tile to ensure complete coverage and to remove excess.

Sponge off haze.

INSTALLING CARPET

Seaming iron

Edge trimmer

Power stretcher

Extension tubes

Knee kicker

Row cutter

Carpet generally requires less preparation for installation than other flooring materials do. The subfloor must be dry, free of debris, and relatively smooth. If you're replacing existing carpet, replace the pad. Carpet pad is relatively inexpensive, and the old one may harbor mildew, mold, and odors. You might be able to reuse tackless strip that's in good condition.

If you have radiant heating, be careful when nailing down tackless strip—you might puncture a pipe. Locate the pipes first by spraying water on the surface along the edge of the wall where the tackless strip will go. Then turn up the heat. Mark the areas that dry first; that's where your radiant heating pipes are. Transfer the marks to the wall or make a precise diagram of the pattern of the piping so you can avoid nailing there.

When you bring the carpet home, store it on a clean surface in a dry area. If the surface is damp, lay a sheet of plastic underneath the carpet roll. Cut the carpet to rough size on a large, clean, dry surface, such as the floor of a large, empty room, a garage floor, or even the driveway that's been swept clean. Then carry the pieces separately into the rooms where they will be installed. Roll and unroll carpet in the direction of the pile.

Weight and bulk make carpet awkward to handle—you may need a helper. One good way to carry a large unrolled piece of carpet is to fold both long sides toward the center and then loosely roll it up. The shorter roll is bulky but easier to maneuver.

PREPARING A FLOOR FOR CARPET

Preparation for conventional and cushion-backed carpet is much the same. This chart notes where additional smoothing is needed for cushion-backed carpet.

Existing Floor	Preparation
Exposed joists	Install ¾-in. T&G CDX/PTS plywood subfloor. Fill nail holes and joints and sand smooth.
Bare concrete	Level and smooth surface.
Wood subfloor	
Over wood frame	Repair surface as needed. If subfloor is rough or gapped, install ⅜- or ½-in. underlayment. For cushion-backed carpet, fill and sand.
Over concrete slab	Remove all wood materials to expose slab, then level and smooth slab.
Wood finish floor	
Over wood frame	Repair surface as needed. For cushion-backed carpet on rough floor, remove floor and install underlayment. Fill and sand.
Over concrete slab	Remove all wood materials to expose slab. Level and smooth slab.
Resilient sheet or tile	
Over wood frame	If existing material is cushioned and loose, remove it. Repair surface or install ⅜- or ½-in. underlayment. For cushion-backed carpet, fill and sand. If existing material is not cushioned but is loose, install ⅜- or ½-in. underlayment. For cushion-backed carpet, fill and sand. If resilient flooring is smooth and tightly bonded, repair surface as needed. For cushion-backed carpet, remove wax and roughen surface.
Over concrete	Repair surface as needed.
Ceramic tile Over wood frame	Remove existing tile, if possible. Repair surface and level it with liquid underlayment. If tile is smooth and tightly bonded, level the surface with a liquid underlayment. Otherwise remove tile and repair surface.
Over concrete slab	For cushion-backed carpet, liquid underlayment must be compatible with carpet adhesive.
Carpet Over wood frame	Remove existing carpet and pad. Repair surface as needed. If subfloor is rough, uneven, or gapped, install ⅜- or ½-in. underlayment.
Over concrete slab	Remove existing carpet and pad. Repair surface as needed.

INSTALLING CONVENTIONAL CARPET

Carpet installation requires a number of steps, but the job is straightforward. You don't have to draw layout lines on the floor, but doing some planning on paper helps, especially in deciding where to locate seams. (See the illustration on the opposite page.) See page 77 for information on preparing the subfloor.

TACKLESS STRIP

Start the job by laying tackless strip—thin pieces of wood with tack points embedded in them. The sharp points grip the carpet, but they will also easily prick your hands and fingers; wear leather gloves for this job.

Starting in one corner, nail the strips around the perimeter of the room with the points angled toward the wall. Leave a gap between the strip and wall that is two-thirds the carpet thickness. Cut strip sections with tin snips and fasten each section with at least two nails. Follow all the angles around door casings or trim.

At doorways in a slab room, nail down a gripper edge with concrete nails. When the flange is hammered down over the carpet, it will bind the carpet edge and makes a clean-looking transition. If you do not want a visible strip, use a Z-bar binding. Nail it under a length of tackless strip installed in the door opening. The carpet wraps over the Z, which then clinches it. (See Transitions, page 81.)

Staple carpet pad to the floor after you install tackless strip around the edge of the room.

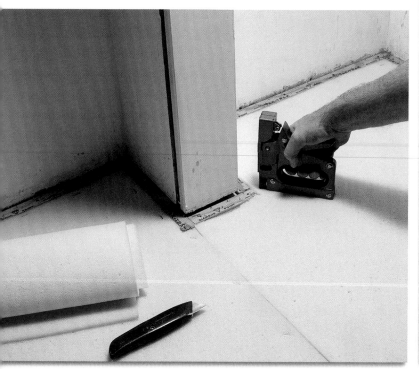

INSTALLING THE PAD

Cut a piece of pad long enough to cover the room from one end to the other. (A utility knife cuts pad easily.) Butt one end of the pad and its edge against the edge of the tackless strip. At the other end, overlap the strip slightly. Staple the pad every 6 to 12 inches around its edges on a wood floor. On a slab, tape the edges down with double-faced carpet tape. Butt the next piece against the first.

Tape the seams with duct tape. Trim the pad back ¼ inch from the tackless strips to keep it from riding on top of the strips when you stretch the carpet. Snap a chalk line on the pad at any seam locations.

CHOOSING A CARPET PAD

Carpet pad is one of the keys to carpeting success. It adds to the resilience of the carpet itself, insulates the floor from temperature changes and noise, provides additional comfort, and can add to the life of the carpet when chosen to match the characteristics of the carpet. Because the pad is the foundation for your carpet, you want one that is firm and resilient.

THE FOUR CARPET PAD MATERIALS:

■ **POLYURETHANE FOAM:** prime foam, like that used in car seats and mattresses.

■ **BONDED POLYURETHANE:** chopped and shredded pieces of scrap polyurethane bonded into a solid piece, often with a reinforcing netting for a backing.

■ **RUBBER:** made from a blend of natural and synthetic rubber, either flat or waffled.

■ **FIBER:** fiber pads may be natural (animal hair and jute) or synthetic (polypropylene, nylon, and acrylics).

Be sure to check with your distributor so you get the pad that matches your carpet style, fibers, and uses. The thickness of the pad you need depends in part on the traffic the carpet will bear. In light traffic areas such as bedrooms and dens, use thicker and softer pads; use a thinner one in high-traffic areas such as living rooms and hallways.

CUTTING THE RUG

■ Cut loop-pile carpet from the front. Clear a cutting path on the pile side using a screwdriver, then cut it with the face side up, using a row cutter or a utility knife.

■ Cut other carpets from the back. Measure the length along both edges on the face side. Mark the cutting points. Roll back the carpet, and snap a chalk line across the back between the marks. Using a straightedge, cut with a utility knife just deep enough to sever the backing. Cut the pile yarn as you separate the pieces.

ROUGH-CUT THE CARPET

Fold the end of the carpet back 3 or 4 feet with the sides lined up to square the end. Measure from the corners to the fold at both sides. If the measurements are not equal, mark the long side at a point equal to the short side. Cut at the mark.

Cut sections for the room with a 4- to 6-inch surplus on each wall. If you have multiple sections, make sure the pile runs the same way. Overlap the seams 3 inches.

Square the carpet in the room and cut vertical slits at corners and obstructions so it lies flat. Seam and stretch the carpet next.

TACKLESS TIPS

Nail tackless strip to wood subfloors. Use masonry nails on concrete, but first drive a few test nails around the perimeter to make sure the concrete will hold them. If the nails don't hold, glue the strip to the slab. Use glue on ceramic tiles too, but roughen the tile surface first. Double-strip where you think one strip won't hold.

If the carpet is going over resilient materials that are laid on concrete, use long nails to get a good bite into the slab. Or remove a 2-inch strip of the flooring at the edges and nail a thicker strip to the slab.

CARPET LAYOUT TIPS

6-in. surplus at wall

3-in. overlap for seam

23 ft.

7 ft. 8 in.

D

Dimensions of 12-ft. carpet when laid

12 ft. 11 ft. 3 in.

Cut

C

A

Direction of nap

B

2 ft. 9 in.

24 ft.

9 ft.

33 ft.

Diagram the carpet, noting cuts for seams. Allow 3-in. overlap on each side of seams and 6-in. surplus at each wall. When cut, the 12×33-foot carpet shown will fit the room with enough surplus for seams and edges.

A

11 ft. 3 in.

7 ft. 8 in.

2 ft. 9 in.

D C B

INSTALLING TACKLESS STRIP AND PAD

Gripper edge or threshold

Tackless strip

Pad

Tape

Cut tackless strip with shears.

Staple pad to subfloor or tape to slab.

Cut pad along straightedge ¼ in. from tackless strip.

INSTALLING CONVENTIONAL CARPET
continued

SEAMING THE CARPET

To cut seams for any carpet, first align the pieces with their edges parallel and the pile of both pieces running in the same direction. Overlap the edge at least 3 inches.

■ To cut loop-pile carpet, use the edge of the top piece as a guide and cut the bottom piece with a row cutter. Finish the cut with a utility knife at the edges where the carpet laps up the wall.

■ For other carpets, fold back the overlap at the seams. Snap a chalk line at equal distances on both edges and cut the seam line with a utility knife and straightedge. Cut the seam edges on both pieces perfectly straight and parallel. If the seam is in a doorway or other location where exact placement is necessary, stretch the first piece of carpet into place before trimming and seaming.

■ Cut hot-melt seaming tape to the exact length of the seam. Lift one of the seam edges and slide the tape into place, centering it on the floor under the seam—adhesive side up. Now warm up the seaming iron.

■ Slip the seaming iron onto the tape at one end of the carpet and let both pieces of carpet flop on top of the iron. Glide the iron along the tape, going about 1 foot every 30 seconds. Press the carpet edges tightly together along each just-heated section.

■ Move the iron with one hand while holding the edges together with the other. Keep the pile out of the adhesive and check to make sure that the backings butt tightly together. As you move away from each heated section, place books or other flat heavy objects on the seam to press it.

■ Continue seaming until you get as close as possible to the far wall. Then stop and let the seamed carpet cool for 5 or 10 minutes so you won't undo your work when seaming at the wall. Roll the edge back to expose the tape. Heat it and finish the seam. Groom the seam by cutting off stray backing threads and loose pile.

SEAMING CONVENTIONAL CARPET

1. Fold back overlapped edges of seams on both sides of largest carpet section. Snap a chalk line on the reverse of both pieces at seam edge.

2. Cut the seam edge on both pieces with a straightedge and utility knife or row cutter.

3. Pull back short edges of small sections, mark seam lines, then cut. Don't cut the long seam until the pieces are joined.

Straightedge

Chalk line for seam on subfloor

Chalk lines mark seam-line cut

Cut line for seam

4. Cut pieces of hot-glue seam tape to length and center them under the seam.

Seaming tape

ROUGH CUTTING CARPET TO FIT THE ROOM

1. Unroll the carpet in the room, orienting the pile in each section in the same direction. Notch the corners so it lays flat.

2. Measure carpet for seam cuts and notch the edges at the measurements.

3. Fold back the carpet to the notches, snap a chalk line between them, then cut with a utility knife or row cutter.

Notch corners to lay material flat.

Seam overlap

6-in. surplus at walls

3-in. overlap at seam

4. Pull all pieces square to the room and lay them out as they will be installed. Make sure that you have the sections to be seamed lined up over the seam chalkline on the subfloor. Overlap the seam edges 3 in.

When you're done, your rough fit should look something like this.

5. Seam the smaller pieces first. Set the seaming iron under the carpet, and when the glue liquifies, draw the iron slowly toward you. Press down on the carpet behind the seaming iron. Weight the seam down until the glue sets.

Seaming iron

Bricks and board

6. When smaller pieces are joined, repeat steps to cut and seam them to the larger piece.

TRANSITIONS

Gripper edge   Metal strip   Binding strip

Hardwood threshold

Transitions ease the passage from one material to another, and the type of transition you use depends on the adjoining materials.

Install a gripper edge on concrete slabs where the adjoining floor is at the same height or lower than the carpet. A reducer strip provides a slightly more stylish transition to a lower floor. For a hidden edge, install a Z-bar binding strip. It becomes invisible when you fasten the carpet to it. Join carpets on the same plane with hot-melt tape or a narrow hardwood threshold.

INSTALLING CONVENTIONAL CARPET
continued

STRETCHING

Before you bring out the stretching tools, decide which wall you're going to start with. It's usually best to start in a corner where an entrance is. Adjust the bite of the knee kicker and power stretcher so the teeth grab the carpet backing; the teeth should not go through the backing.

STRETCHING CONVENTIONAL CARPET

Tail block

Teeth grab carpet backing.

Knee kicker

Pad   Subfloor

2×4 spanning 2 or 3 studs

Push down handle to set stretcher.

Power stretcher

Kick swiftly with knee.

1 to 3 in. from wall

6 in. from wall, 24 in. from corners

Tuck carpet at edge with stair tool.

Head piece

To secure the carpet onto the tackless strip, bite the head of the kicker into the carpet about 1 inch from the wall. Push down on the handle and swiftly kick the cushion with your knee. Proceed kick by kick, holding the secured carpet down on the strip with your hand or with a stair tool so it won't unhook.

Follow the kicking and stretching sequence illustrated in the diagram on the opposite page. For short distances (across hallways or small bedrooms, for example), use the knee kicker. In larger rooms, use a power stretcher.

Set the head of the power stretcher 6 inches from the wall and adjust the extension tubes so that the foot presses against the opposite wall (support the foot with a carpet-covered 2×4 that spans 2 or

3 studs). Then press down on the lever to stretch the carpet toward the wall. The lever should lock down with a gentle push.

If the carpet does not move easily, lift the head and lower the handle a bit before biting into the carpet again. With the handle locked and the carpet stretched, fasten the edge of the carpet to the tackless strip with the side of a hammer or the trowel-like paddle that comes with the stretcher. Push the carpet down onto the pins. Then release the stretcher head, move it over 18 inches, and repeat the process. Move the foot of the stretcher along the opposite wall as you go.

TRIMMING

Trim the carpet edges with a wall trimmer. Adjust the trimmer to the thickness of the carpet. Start at the lapped end of the carpet and slice downward at an angle until the trimmer is flat against the floor. Then hold the trimmer against both the wall and the floor and plow it along the edge of the carpet.

Carefully trim the last few inches with a utility knife. Using a stair tool, tuck the trimmed carpet edge down between the tackless strip and the baseboard. Position the tool on the surplus carpet that laps over the gap, rather than out on the edge of the carpet itself. That keeps the carpet from bulging back and lifting off the pins. Hit the stair tool with a rubber mallet if the carpet is stiff.

At doorways, trim the edge of the carpet to the center of the closed door. If you installed a gripper edge on a concrete floor, flatten the metal flange over the carpet with a rubber mallet or a wood block and hammer. If the edge of the carpet will be covered with a metal flat bar, nail it down first with tacks or 1-inch lath nails.

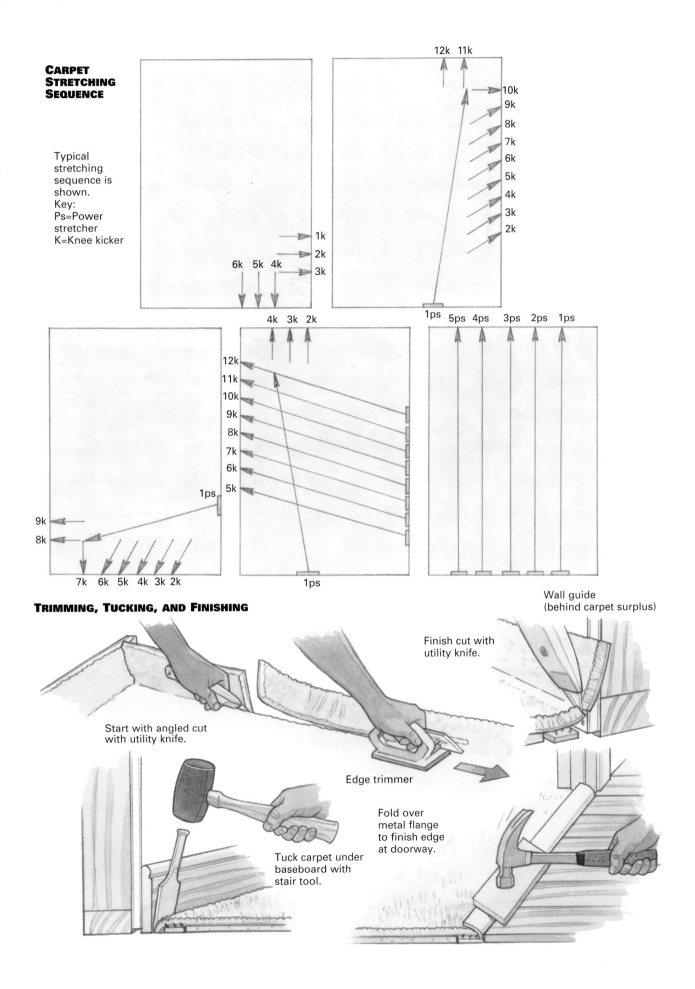

CARPET STRETCHING SEQUENCE

Typical stretching sequence is shown.
Key:
Ps=Power stretcher
K=Knee kicker

TRIMMING, TUCKING, AND FINISHING

Start with angled cut with utility knife.

Edge trimmer

Finish cut with utility knife.

Wall guide (behind carpet surplus)

Tuck carpet under baseboard with stair tool.

Fold over metal flange to finish edge at doorway.

INSTALLING CUSHION-BACKED CARPET

Cushion-backed carpet has its own bonded foam backing, but since it's thin, it will show the smallest imperfection. You won't need to stretch this carpet; just glue it to the floor. First make sure the floor is properly prepared according to the information on pages 44–47.

Don't remove the baseboards before installing cushion-backed carpet. The carpet edges will be tucked under them during trimming. At doorways, install a toothless binder bar with a flange that clamps down over the carpet to finish the edge.

VENTILATE THE ROOM

Some carpet adhesives are noxious or even flammable. Read the manufacturer's instructions carefully, and make sure that the room is well ventilated. Extinguish nearby pilot lights and other open flames before using adhesives.

Carpeting adds warmth and comfort to this cheery sitting room. The deep blue color complements the pale yellow walls.

ROUGHING IT IN

If your carpet will be seamed, snap a chalk line on the floor where a seam will fall. Then, whether seamed or not, rough-cut (face side up) the carpet with a 6-inch excess at the walls. If you're seaming, carefully align one edge of the piece on the chalk line. Place the second piece so that its edge overlaps the bottom one by ¼ inch. Be sure that the pattern, if any, lines up and that the pile of both pieces runs in the same direction.

SEAMING THE CARPET

At the seam, fold both edges back 2 or 3 feet and trowel a thin, even coat of adhesive onto the exposed floor. Roll one edge back down so it's exactly on the chalk line. Work the carpet with your hands to force air bubbles out to the edge.

Notch the seaming-fluid nozzle so it will apply a bead of adhesive at the height of the primary backing, not onto the pile or pad. Lay a bead of seaming fluid along the edge of the primary backing material on the piece of carpet that's glued to the floor.

Fold the second piece of carpet so that its edge tightly abuts the edge of the adhered piece. The edges should press tightly together because you allowed a ¼-inch overlap. Work the bulge produced by the ¼-inch allowance gently away from the seam. Where there are gaps, carefully rejoin both edges with your fingers until the entire seam is tight. Let the adhesive dry thoroughly, then snip off loose pile or backing threads.

GLUING

Pull the carpet from the side walls and fold in the corners. Then pull the whole piece back to the seam area. (If the carpet didn't require a seam, pull the single piece back until half the floor is exposed.) Trowel adhesive onto the floor and roll the carpet from the center to the wall. Work out wrinkles or bumps with your hands as you go. Repeat the process for the other half of the carpet. If you have to deflate a bubble, pierce it with an awl. Use a plastic syringe (available from carpet dealers) to inject contact adhesive into the hole. Press the carpet firmly onto the adhesive.

TRIMMING

Trim the carpet with a utility knife. Leave a margin equal to the thickness of the carpet and tuck it down against the wall with a stair tool. Flatten down any metal doorway flanges with a hammer and a block of wood.

INSTALLING CUSHION-BACKED CARPET

1. Snap a chalk line at the location of any seam. Roll out the first section, leaving a 6-inch surplus at the walls. Line up one edge at the seam line.

2. Roll out the second piece so it overlaps the first by ¼ inch evenly along the seam length. Leave a 6-inch surplus at the walls.

3. Fold back both edges 2 to 3 feet from the line and trowel on a thin, even adhesive coat to the folded edges.

4. Fold the bottom piece back on the adhesive, keeping its edge exactly on the chalk line. Lay a bead of seaming fluid along the edge of the carpet backing, not on the pile or cushion.

5. Fold the second piece so its edge butts tightly against the first piece. Make sure the pattern lines up and gently work out the bulge back to the edge of the adhesive.

6. Fold back one half of the carpet to the adhesive line. Spread adhesive to the wall and roll carpet back on adhesive, working out wrinkles as you go.

7. Seat the carpet edge at the wall with a stair tool. Trim excess and retuck.

CLEANING, MAINTENANCE, AND REPAIR

REPLACING DAMAGED STRIP OR PLANK FLOORING

1. *Using a square, mark the damaged section.*

2. *Drill the damaged section with a ⅜-in. spade bit just to the inside edges of the marks.*

3. *Plunge-cut the section with a saw set to the depth of the flooring.*

4. *Chisel out the cut section.*

5. *Square drilled edge with a sharp chisel, bevel facing the edge.*

6. *Cut replacement board, removing bottom edge of groove.*

7. *Tap replacements into place, toenailing where possible and gluing if necessary. Remove bottom of groove.*

MAINTAINING WOOD FLOORS

Modern wood finishes can stand up to more abuse than could finishes of 50 years ago. But, just as was true 50 years ago, floors still need to be cleaned regularly.

Cleaning techniques for floors with surface finishes and waxed floors are slightly different. To tell if your floor is waxed, drop a little water in an out-of-the-way corner. If white spots appear after about 10 minutes, the floor is waxed. Remove the white spots by buffing with #0000 steel wool and a little wax.

SURFACE FINISHES: Dust or vacuum the floor regularly. Clean spills immediately, using a dampened—not saturated—cloth. Clean the floor with a general-purpose floor cleaner or a product recommended by the finish manufacturer. Urethane-finished floors don't need wax—it will just make the floor slippery. A dulled urethane finish may need sanding and a recoat. Some urethanes can be recoated without sanding.

WAXED FLOORS: Dust or vacuum regularly. After taking up spills with a dampened—but not saturated—cloth, buff with a soft, dry cloth to return the shine. Buff only the dull areas of the floor. Clean the floor once a year with a solvent-based cleaner (water-based cleaners will fog the finish). Then wax and buff the floor.

BASIC WOOD-FLOOR REPAIRS

Wood floors may become damaged occasionally. A split, crack, or moisture damage in one area can usually be repaired without tearing up the floor. Some damage may be confined to the surface or finish; refer to the chart on the opposite page for advice about repairing surface damage to solid-wood floors. Replacing damaged sections of wood flooring is fairly straightforward; the illustrations on these two pages will lead you through the steps.

REPLACING DAMAGED PARQUET TILE

1. Plunge-cut the damaged tile with a circular saw set to the thickness of the parquet.

2. Place the bevel of a butt chisel toward the edge of the cuts and remove the cut pieces. Scrape up the remaining adhesive with a putty knife.

3. Cut bottom edges of the groove, spread adhesive on the subfloor, set the new tile into place, and tap it down.

FIXING WARPED BOARDS

1. Remove wax or finish with appropriate solvent. Cover warped boards with damp rags for 48 hours.

2. Predrill and countersink holes, then screw the warped boards to subfloor. Keeping the flooring damp, tighten the screws a little each day until the board is flat.

3. Let the flooring dry completely, then fill the holes and refinish to match original finish.

WOOD SURFACE REPAIRS

Problem	Remedy
Bubbles in finish	May be caused by incompatible finishes. For light damage, sand lightly and recoat. If heavy, sand, stain, and refinish.
Chewing gum, crayon, candle wax	Pop off with ice in a bag, scrape with plastic scraper. Seep cleaning fluid under chewing gum.
Cigarette burns	Burnish with fine steel wool or scrape charred area. Wax, or sand, stain, and refinish.
Dents	Cover with dampened cloth and press with an electric iron.
Scratches	Wax the area or hide the scratch with a thin coat of dusting spray rubbed into scratch.
Seasonal cracks	Increase humidity in dry season—install humidifier, boil water, open dishwasher after rinse.
Surface stains	Remove with sandpaper or steel wool, feathering edges; or clean with one of these solutions:
Heel marks	Wood cleaner or wax.
Oil and grease	Try wood cleaner first. Then, on waxed floor, use TSP or soap with high lye content. On surface finish, use TSP.
Pet stains	Wood cleaner, followed by mild bleach or household vinegar for up to an hour. A remaining spot is not likely to sand out. Cover damage with rug or remove, replace, and refinish.
Ink	Use same procedure as for pet stains.
Mold, mildew	Floor cleaner. If wood fibers are stained, remove and refinish.
Water spots	Buff lightly with #0000 steel wool, then wax. If necessary, sand with fine paper, stain, and recoat.

REFINISHING WOOD FLOORS

Refinishing a solid-wood floor is a time-consuming and exacting process. Before you start sanding your floor, first determine if the floor needs refinishing; you might just need to recondition it. Then pull off a floor vent to make sure you have sufficient wood left to sand. Standard ¾-inch flooring can be sanded a number of times, but if yours has only slightly more than ½ inch left, you should consult a floor contractor. The same applies to manufactured flooring; it's even thinner, so sanding it is definitely a job for the pros.

SANDING A WOOD FLOOR

Pad sander

Stop sander before sanding cross-grain at borders.

Fan exhausts dust to outside.

Door taped shut to keep dust out of the house.

Remove baseboards

1. Start sanding about two-thirds of the way along the length of the room on the right side. Sand with the grain.

2. Push sander forward; at wall, move it left a few inches and pull it back to the starting point.

3. After sanding to the side wall, turn sander in the opposite direction and repeat the process, overlapping the starting point by the width of the sanding pad.

Use an edge sander along the walls and in other areas the pad sander won't reach. Sand with a circular motion along the wall, overlapping into the area removed by the pad sander.

TIP-TOP REFINISHING

When you are refinishing a solid wood floor, you're going to have your hands full (of heavy equipment, for one thing). Here are a few tips that will make the job go smoothly.

■ Sanding should remove less than ¹⁄₃₂ inch. Because the surface of manufactured flooring is relatively thin, refinishing a manufactured floor should be done by a professional.

■ Grits—Very coarse (20 to 30), coarse (36 to 40), medium (50 to 80), fine (100, 120), very fine (150). Use coarse grits only on rough floors. If medium grit will level the floor on the first cut, don't use coarse grit.

■ Immediately mark nails, hollows, and depressions as you sand.

■ Don't skip more than one grade between grits (you can skip from 30 to 40, but not from 30 to 50).

RECONDITIONING A WOOD FLOOR

If you don't change the color of your floor or if damage is superficial, you may only need to recondition it. Reconditioning a wood floor means removing or lightly sanding only the finish of the floor. First, find out if you have a surface finish or not—scrape lightly in a corner. Flakes tell you it's a surface finish. No flakes mean it's a penetrant. In either case, check for wax by dropping a little water on the floor. If the beads turn white after 10 minutes, it's waxed and will have to be sanded and refinished. No wax means you can coat over it. Clean the floor with a cleaner that won't leave a residue, dull the sheen with steel wool or a sanding screen, then coat with a compatible finish. Don't finish a floor with shellac or lacquer—the first is not durable, and the second is extremely flammable.

CHOOSING FINISHES

Wood finishes fall into two categories—penetrating and surface finishes.

■ Penetrants go into the wood pores. They don't wear off unless the wood does; you can retouch them and the floor won't look patched. There are two types of penetrants:

Stains—if you want a color in your wood other than its natural color, start with stain. Protect stain with a penetrating sealer or surface finish.

Sealers—these come either clear or tinted (making staining and sealing a one-step process). Protect sealers with a wax or surface finish.

■ Surface finishes set up on the surface of the wood, providing a harder and more durable coating than sealers. Here's a summary of their characteristics:

Urethane (oil-modified)—Easy to apply, dries slowly, amber color, very durable.

Urethane (water-based)—Easy to apply, dries fast, clear. More durable than oil-modified urethanes.

Urethane (moisture-cured)—Difficult to apply, dries quickly in presence of moisture, clear to amber. Most durable of the urethanes.

Almost all finishes will discolor over time, and some need protection from UV light (drape the windows). If you use area rugs, wait until the finish has cured—about two weeks for water-based urethane, a month for solvent-based finishes. Purchase rugs with backing that will let the floor breathe and won't react with the finish.

APPLYING FINISH TO A WOOD FLOOR

Using a wide-blade putty knife, fill cracks with a paste filler. Push the filler into the wood at an angle to the grain. Sand the filler with medium- and fine-grit paper.

Following the manufacturer's directions and using a lamb's wool applicator or brush, start in one corner of the room and work in the direction of the flooring. Apply a liberal amount of finish with the grain and work from unfinished areas to the edge that is still wet. Always leave a wet edge, feathering new finish into it on the next pass.

FINISHING STEPS

To refinish (or finish an unfinished floor), refer to the illustrations at top right and follow the steps below. Use an orbital pad sander instead of a drum sander—the pad sander takes off less wood, is less likely to make gouges, and is more forgiving of error.

■ Remove furniture, shoe moldings, vents, and protruding nails. Vacuum thoroughly.

■ Load the sander with coarse or medium paper; coarse if removing a surface or waxed finish or if the floor is rough.

■ To make the first pass, start at the right-hand wall, about two-thirds of the way from the end wall. Walk the sander toward the end wall, then walk it back on the same path. At the starting point, move the sander over 3 to 4 inches and repeat the process. Continue sanding, overlapping paths until you've sanded two-thirds of the room. Then face the other end wall and repeat the process; overlap the starting edge 2 to 3 feet.

■ Sand the edges with an edge sander (with the same or next finer grit) parallel to the

wall, moving in a quarter-circle pattern and overlapping the sanded area 4 to 6 inches.

■ Make the second pass. Repeat sanding and edging with the next finer grit.

■ Make the third pass. Fill nail holes and repeat sanding with fine paper.

■ Smooth corners with a scraper and sand with a small power orbital sander.

■ Vacuum thoroughly and remove fine dust by going over the entire floor carefully with a tack cloth.

■ Apply stain and finish of your choice.

REFINISHING PARQUET

Parquet refinishing follows the same procedures outlined above, with one exception—the sanding pattern. Make the first two passes along opposite diagonals and the third one parallel to the long wall in the room.

MAINTAINING RESILIENT AND LAMINATE FLOORS

REPAIRING RESILIENT SHEET FLOORING

1. *Cut a piece of sheet material larger than the damaged area. Tape it over the damaged area with its pattern matching the rest of the floor exactly.*

2. *Using a utility knife and straightedge, cut through both pieces.*

3. *Pull off the patch and tape, then warm the area with a hair dryer. Remove the damaged area and adhesive with a putty knife. Apply adhesive to the floor and replace with new material. Weight it until the adhesive cures.*

Caring for your resilient or laminate floor mostly involves keeping it clean. Regular sweeping or vacuuming will take care of most of the grit, but should be accompanied by periodic sponge-mopping with a mild solution of ammonia. Don't flood the surface.

Avoid abrasive cleaners or applicators that might scratch the floor. If you're in doubt about what cleaner is compatible with your resilient or laminate surface, contact the dealer; most flooring manufacturers market cleaning agents that are compatible with their floor materials.

The no-wax surface on resilient sheet and tiles makes cleaning easier, but be sure to use cleaners that are compatible with the material; many are not. One-step cleaners can scratch resilient or laminate flooring. Although the cleaner is supposed to remove dirt, some particles get caught in the applicator and are spread across the floor, where they can continue to abrade its surface.

REMOVING STAINS FROM RESILIENT FLOORING

Stain	Remove with
Asphalt, shoe polish	Citrus-based cleaner or mineral spirits.
Candle wax	Scrape carefully with plastic spatula.
Crayon	Mineral spirits or manufacturer's cleaner.
Grape juice, wine, mustard	Full-strength bleach or manufacturer's cleaner.
Heel marks	Nonabrasive household cleaner. If stain remains, use rubbing alcohol.
Lipstick	Rubbing alcohol or mineral spirits.
Nail polish	Nail polish remover.
Paint or varnish	Water or mineral spirits while still wet. If dry, scrape carefully with a thin plastic spatula. If stain still shows, rub with rubbing alcohol.
Pen ink	Citrus-based cleaner, rubbing alcohol, or mineral spirits.
Permanent marker	Mineral spirits, nail polish remover, or rubbing alcohol.
Rust	Oxalic acid and water (1 part acid to 10 parts water). Extremely caustic; follow all directions.

After removing the stain, rinse the area with a damp cloth to remove residue.

PREVENTING DENTS AND SCRATCHES

Resilient flooring is more prone to dents, scuffs, and scratches than other flooring. Unlike spots, you can't remove them. Here are some ways to prevent dents:
■ Protect the floor when moving appliances. Lay plywood panels on the floor and "walk" the appliance across the panels.
■ Use floor protectors to keep furniture legs from denting the floors; the heavier the furniture, the wider the protector should be.
■ Avoid furniture with rolling casters. If you must have casters, use double rollers.
■ Keep dust and dirt outside the house—use mats or rugs at entrances, but avoid rubber-backed rugs. They can discolor resilient flooring.
■ Keep the floor clean with regular sweeping or vacuuming, but don't use vacuums with beater bars—or any abrasive scrubbing aids. They can scratch the floor.

REFINISHING

The finish needs to be renewed periodically on resilient floors that don't have a no-wax surface. Clear acrylic products are suitable for this purpose. Periodic removal and restoration of the finish will probably also be necessary.

Laminate floors won't need refinishing, but if the shine begins to dull, renew it with the product specified by the manufacturer.

STAIN REMOVAL TECHNIQUES

If your flooring becomes stained, first attempt to clean it with soap and water on a soft cloth or a nylon nonabrasive pad. Never use abrasive applicators. For more stubborn stains, work up to liquid floor cleaner, rubbing (isopropyl) alcohol, diluted chlorine bleach, or mineral spirits. Use the cleaner recommended on the charts on these pages, if the stain is shown.

Regardless of the cleaner, work at the edges of the stain first, and change the surface of the cloth so you're not spreading the stain into unstained areas.

MAKING REPAIRS

From time to time, the inevitable happens— your floor becomes damaged to the point that repairs are necessary. Although you can repair laminate dents, chips, and scratches with a repair kit available from your dealer (see the illustration at right), leave substantial repairs and those that require removal and replacement of a plank to a professional.

Resilient materials are easier to repair. Repairing sheet flooring involves cutting out the damaged section and gluing in a patch of the same size and pattern. A damaged resilient tile can be removed, then replaced with a new tile, as shown at right. Both processes are well within the skill level of the average homeowner.

Although the wearlayer of laminate floors is extremely hard, small dents are bound to occur eventually. Flooring dealers sell a dent repair kit with a filler that hardens to a resistant surface and matches the color of the flooring. The illustration above shows a typical repair procedure. Replace damaged resilient tiles as shown at right.

LAMINATE FLOORING STAIN REMOVAL GUIDE

Stain	Remove with
Candle wax	Scrape carefully with plastic spatula.
Crayon, rubber heel marks	Rub out with a dry cloth or acetone if needed.
Grape juice or wine	Rub with a dry cloth or concentrated cleaner.
Lipstick	Paint thinner or acetone.
Nail polish	Acetone-based nail polish remover.
Paint or varnish	Wipe with water or mineral spirits while still wet. If dry, scrape carefully with a thin plastic spatula. If the stain still shows, rub with rubbing alcohol.
Pen ink	Acetone or paint thinner.
Shoe polish	Acetone or paint thinner.
Tar	Acetone.
Others	Start with concentrated cleaner, then acetone.

After removing the stain, rinse the area with a damp cloth to remove residue.

REPAIRING LAMINATE FLOORING

1. Clean the area; when dry, protect the surrounding surfaces with clear plastic tape.

2. Fill the dent with putty from flooring repair kit. Wipe up the excess with a cloth dampened with the recommended solvent. Remove tape.

REPAIRING RESILIENT TILE

1. Remove damaged tile and adhesive with a putty knife, softening tiles with a hair dryer.

2. Spread adhesive and lay in new tile.

MAINTAINING CERAMIC TILE

REPLACING GROUT

1. Dig out grout with a grout saw.

2. Apply new grout with a float. Smooth and wipe off excess and haze.

REPLACING BROKEN TILE

2. Remove chips with a chisel or putty knife. Scrape adhesive.

3. Apply adhesive to tile and floor.

4. Tap tile into place, let dry, then grout joint.

1. Score grout and break tile with a hammer.

Ceramic tile requires less maintenance than most other home flooring materials. Regular mopping and vacuuming are musts, of course. Glazed tiles resist stains better than stone and unglazed tile. Grout shows stains.

REMOVING STAINS FROM TILE

Stains	Cleaner and Method
Grease, fats	Clean with a commercial spot lifter.
Ink, coffee, blood, mustard, fruit juice, and some dyes	Start with a 3-percent hydrogen peroxide solution; if that doesn't work, try a nonbleach cleaner.
Nail polish	Use nail polish remover.
Oil-base products	Mild solvent, such as charcoal lighter or mineral spirits, then household cleaner in a poultice. For dried paint, scrape with a plastic (not metal) scraper.
Rust	Use commercial rust removers made for fabric, then household cleaner.

Rinse the area with a damp cloth to remove residue.

SEALING TILE

Unglazed tile usually requires sealing. Although many come from the factory presealed, periodic resealing may be necessary. Sealers come in two varieties:

■ Sealers penetrate tile to preserve its natural color and keep stains out of the pores.
■ Topical sealers lay on top of the tile. Depending on the sealer, they can lighten, darken, or change the sheen of an unsealed tile. Topical sealers wear faster and require more frequent application.

CLEANING TIPS

In addition to regular sweeping or vacuuming, periodic damp-mopping with a neutral-pH cleaner will keep both glazed and sealed, unglazed tiles looking good.

If you need to scrub something stubborn, don't use steel wool or metal tools. Metal will leave residue behind and there's almost nothing that will remove these marks. Use nylon scrubbers or brushes with plastic or natural bristles—a toothbrush for grout. Check the chart above for stain-removing tips.

STAINS ON STONE

A poultice—a mixture of plaster of Paris and hydrogen peroxide wrapped in a soft cloth—or one of the cleaners listed in the chart above can pull stains out of the pores of stone tile. This is a slow process. Spread the poultice mixture over the stain and tape plastic over it. Let it sit for a couple of days, then brush it off. Ask your dealer what cleaning products to use for your stone.

CARPET MAINTENANCE

Carpet—unlike other flooring materials—can look clean when it isn't. That's because dirt particles work their way down from the surface and into the fabric. They do more damage there than when they're visible on top; they abrade the fabric fibers when you walk on the carpet.

Vacuum once or twice a week. Use a quality vacuum cleaner that's in good repair—and empty the bag. The vacuum is less efficient with a full bag.

Even if you stick to a rigorous vacuuming schedule, clean your carpet periodically to restore it to brand-new condition.

CLEANING METHODS

There are a number of effective cleaning methods that you can hire done or do yourself with rented equipment. Some methods use brushes, some don't. Brushes can distort the pile of some carpets.

DRY EXTRACTION: An absorbent compound with detergents is brushed into the fabric with specially designed machines. The compound attaches to the dirt, and both are picked up by the vacuum.

DRY FOAM: Detergent foam is worked into the fibers by machine brushes and either wet-vacuumed or allowed to dry before being vacuumed up.

HOT WATER EXTRACTION (STEAM CLEANING): Cleaning solution is injected into the carpet under pressure and immediately taken out. This method doesn't use brushes, so it's good for pile that can be untwisted by brushes. Be careful; it's easy to over-wet the carpet, which can cause the backing to shrink or mildew to grow.

ROTARY SHAMPOO: Cleaning solution is injected into the carpet, worked by machine brushes, then vacuumed out when dry. This is the kind of machine you can usually rent at grocery stores and other outlets. Use the least amount of detergent possible to keep residue

TIPS FOR CARPET CLEANING

Your do-it-yourself cleaning efforts will go more smoothly with the following precautions.
- Prevacuum to remove as much soil as possible.
- Before cleaning, use a preconditioning agent to loosen the soil—then let it work for about 10 minutes.
- Remove all the furniture that you can. Put plastic film around the legs of big pieces to keep them from getting damaged and to prevent rust stains on the carpet.
- Ventilate the room with fans to speed drying.
- Make sure the carpet is dry before walking on it.

STAIN REMOVAL GUIDE FOR CARPETS

When removing stains with any of the following methods, act quickly and blot the area. Do not scrub—it can distort the carpet pile and spread the stain. Formulas for ammonia, detergent, and vinegar solutions are at the bottom right of page 94.

Stain	Removal
Alcoholic beverages and soft drinks	Detergent solution, ammonia solution, or white vinegar solution.
Blood	Always use spot removing solutions cold to avoid setting the stain. Start with an ammonia solution, then try detergent solution, white vinegar solution, and warm water rinse.
Burns	Reweaving or resectioning are about the only cures for burn damage. Clipping the fabric just below the burn can improve its appearance.
Candle wax	Nail polish remover or dry-cleaning fluid.
Chocolate	Dry-cleaning fluid, detergent solution, ammonia solution, or white vinegar solution.
Coffee	Detergent solution or warm white vinegar solution.
Crayon	Dry-cleaning fluid or detergent solution.
Fingernail polish	Nail polish remover or detergent solution.
Gum	Soften the gum slightly with a hair dryer (don't melt the carpet). Lift the gum away with a plastic bag (the softened gum will stick to it). Finish with dry-cleaning fluid.
Ink	Nail polish remover, dry-cleaning fluid, detergent solution, or ammonia solution.
Latex paint	Detergent solution or ammonia solution.
Lipstick	Nail polish remover, dry-cleaning fluid, detergent solution, ammonia solution, or white vinegar solution.
Pet stains	Detergent solution, white vinegar solution or ammonia solution.
Rust	White vinegar solution or detergent solution.
Shoe polish	Nail polish remover, dry-cleaning fluid or detergent solution.

CARPET MAINTENANCE
continued

to a minimum. Dirt sticks to detergent residue, causing the carpet to wear more quickly. Don't use a counter-rotating floor-polishing machine to scrub carpet—you will untwist your carpet pile.

You can use all these cleaning methods on wool, cotton, rayon, and other synthetic carpets, but use only the manufacturer's recommended cleaning solutions.

FOOTPRINTS AND OTHER DEPRESSIONS

Carpet is a soft material, and it will show indentations that hard-surfaced flooring will not. How well a carpet resists these blemishes is determined partly by its density and partly by the method used to make it. Denser carpets usually bounce back more quickly. Here's an overview of some of the more common carpet problems and what (if anything) you can do about them.

CORNROWING is a condition you'll recognize if some of the rows of your carpet begin to stand out and others don't. High-density carpet is less prone to cornrowing because fiber tufts that are packed together tightly tend to support each other, even when stretched apart during installation. Vacuuming generally won't help. Special carpet rakes might help, but not permanently.

CRUSHING is the loss of pile thickness due to normal traffic. Vacuuming will lift the pile, but it can't replace worn fiber.

FADING can be caused by furnace fumes and sunlight. Have your furnace serviced regularly and close the drapes when the room is not in use to minimize fading.

SHEDDING is natural, caused by loose fibers left over from the manufacturing process rising to the surface. It will disappear within a year if you vacuum regularly.

RIPPLES are usually caused by improper stretching or a failed cushion. They can also appear where humidity is high. Have a professional installer remove them by restretching the carpet.

SPROUTING is the sudden appearance of one or two yarns for no apparent reason. Don't pull out carpet sprouts; snip them off at the level of the rest of the tufts.

DENTS caused by furniture can be minimized with wide furniture glides. You can sometimes work them out with your fingers. If that doesn't work, moisten the area, warm it slightly with a hair dryer, and ease the fibers into position with the back of a spoon.

STAIN REMOVAL SOLUTIONS

Modern carpets are manufactured with finishes that resist stains, but that still doesn't make them stainproof. Stain-resistant finishes hold the stain on the carpet's surface so you can remove it before it penetrates deeper.

Respond quickly when something stains your carpet; remove the spot as soon as possible. Blot stains; don't scrub them or you might damage the carpet pile and probably spread the stain.

Using a clean, white, absorbent cloth, gently work in the cleaner from the edges of the spot toward the center. Keep blotting until you can't see the stain on the cloth. Then use clean, warm water to take up the cleaner residue. Blot the excess water from the fibers. Let the carpet dry, then vacuum. If your cleaning efforts aren't successful, you'll have to call a professional cleaner.

Most carpet manufacturers offer a cleaning kit with ingredients that are compatible with their carpet fibers. If you use the manufacturer's kit, you won't have to worry about whether the cleaner will take the color out of the carpet. You can also brew your own cleaners for use with the methods shown in the chart on page 93. Try the methods in the order shown on the chart. Some of the cleaners listed are over-the-counter products like dry-cleaning fluid and nail polish remover. Others are home-brew mixtures. Here are the formulas for those:

■ Mild detergent solution (¼ teaspoon mild liquid detergent to a cup of lukewarm water).

■ Vinegar solution (1 cup white vinegar to 2 cups water).

■ Ammonia solution (2 tablespoons household ammonia to 1 cup water).

VACUUM CLEANER CHECKLIST

If you're shopping for a vacuum cleaner, purchase a model with adjustable and rotating brushes. Make sure it has a strong enough airflow to lift dirt up from the backing and a high-filtration bag to keep the dust contained.

Take these simple steps to help keep your vacuum efficient:
■ Replace worn brushes.
■ Don't vacuum with clogged hoses.
■ Keep a spare belt on hand and change it before it breaks.
■ Change the bag when it's just over half full—as it fills, the vacuum's efficiency decreases.

INDEX

METRIC CONVERSIONS

U.S. Units to Metric Equivalents			Metric Units to U.S. Equivalents		
To Convert From	Multiply By	To Get	To Convert From	Multiply By	To Get
Inches	25.4	Millimeters	Millimeters	0.0394	Inches
Inches	2.54	Centimeters	Centimeters	0.3937	Inches
Feet	30.48	Centimeters	Centimeters	0.0328	Feet
Feet	0.3048	Meters	Meters	3.2808	Feet
Yards	0.9144	Meters	Meters	1.0936	Yards
Square inches	6.4516	Square centimeters	Square centimeters	0.1550	Square inches
Square feet	0.0929	Square meters	Square meters	10.764	Square feet
Square yards	0.8361	Square meters	Square meters	1.1960	Square yards
Acres	0.4047	Hectares	Hectares	2.4711	Acres
Cubic inches	16.387	Cubic centimeters	Cubic centimeters	0.0610	Cubic inches
Cubic feet	0.0283	Cubic meters	Cubic meters	35.315	Cubic feet
Cubic feet	28.316	Liters	Liters	0.0353	Cubic feet
Cubic yards	0.7646	Cubic meters	Cubic meters	1.308	Cubic yards
Cubic yards	764.55	Liters	Liters	0.0013	Cubic yards

To convert from degrees Fahrenheit (F) to degrees Celsius (C), first subtract 32, then multiply by $\frac{5}{9}$.

To convert from degrees Celsius to degrees Fahrenheit, multiply by $\frac{9}{5}$, then add 32.